Cornell International Industrial and Labor Relations Report
Number 10

Working Women in Japan
Discrimination, Resistance, and Reform

Alice H. Cook and Hiroko Hayashi

New York State School of
Industrial and Labor Relations

Cover design by Lauren Kasman

Cover photo from Shin Fujin Shinbun
The sign in the foreground reads: *Sex discrimination in glamorous JAL* [*Japan Air Lines*]. *In our twenties, they pamper us. In our thirties, they exploit us. In our forties, they want to get rid of us.* —JAL Labor Unions, Department of Women

Library of Congress Cataloging in Publication Data
Cook, Alice Hanson
  Working women in Japan.
(Cornell international industrial and labor relations report; no. 10)
  Bibliography: p.
  Includes index.
  1. Women — Employment — Japan. 2. Sex discrimination in employment — Japan. 3. Sex discrimination against women — Japan. I. Hayashi, Hiroko, 1943– joint author. II. Title. III. Series: Cornell international industrial and labor relations reports; no. 10.
HD6197.C66   331.4'133'0952   80-17706
ISBN 0-87546-078-X
ISBN 0-87546-079-8 (pbk.)

Copies may be ordered from
Publications Division
New York State School of
Labor and Industrial Relations
Cornell University
Ithaca, New York 14853

Contents

1.
Women in the Japanese Employment System

Japan's labor force has a higher percentage of women working than any other noncommunist country. Its figures rival those of Sweden and Finland and have remained remarkably steady at 50 to 51 percent of women fifteen years of age and over from 1955 to 1975 (Appendix A gives a detailed statistical description of women's position in the labor force).[1]

Many norms that are used to describe the nature and scope of women's work in the national economies of the industrial nations, however, do not apply to Japan. Whereas in many countries women work after leaving school and until the birth of their first or second child, then remain at home for a few years caring for children and return to work either part or full time, the Japanese employment system makes such a pattern very difficult for women to follow without great loss both in status and income. In most countries a close, positive correlation exists between a woman's level of education and an uninterrupted or only briefly interrupted work life. In Japan, again because of the employment system, women college graduates have the greatest difficulty finding and keeping employment and in receiving wages commensurate with their education. Like many other industrial countries, Japan has established the principle in its law of equal pay of the sexes. Like other countries, the discrepancies between men's and women's earnings are wide, but in Japan they grow wider with the length of employment. Indeed, given the traditional views that most Japanese, male and female, hold about women's roles in the family and at work, the Japanese employment system probably exploits women more extensively than is the case in any other industrialized country.

While the vast majority of women accept these fateful facts, an increasing number of women workers are protesting the discrimination they suffer. The method they are using with telling effect in many cases is legal prosecution of their employers. It is the authors' contention that the increasing number of cases brought by working women to the courts is an index of women's growing self-consciousness and of their determination to achieve the equality that Japan's constitution and statutory law state is theirs. It is the purpose of this book to make clear the significance of the cases that have to be taken to court and to raise the question of whether the decisions being issued, generally favorable as they are, will in fact change the status and role of women in the Japan employment system.

Many authors have tackled the problem of making clear to Western scholars and businesspersons the special nature of the Japanese system. James Abegglen with his *Japanese Factory* was the first.[2] He contended that the lifelong employment system peculiar to Japanese industry in this century, and particularly since World War II, so expressed Japanese social values that it would resist the pressures of industrialism to create uniformity in employment practices on the Western model. Others have elaborated on special aspects of the system.[3] Some scholars have attempted to prove Abegglen wrong. The most recent of these were Robert M. Marsh and Hiroshi Nannari.[4] Along with Robert Dore,[5] they find changes having taken place since the early 1960s that in some aspects appear to bring the paternal lifetime commitment system in Japan closer to Western practice. At the same time they find it difficult to show that the current or long-range developments were actually moving in this direction and had even greater difficulty in detecting fundamental changes in the system. The questions of whether and how the system is changing are of major importance to an examination of women's role within it.

These authors agree that the major characteristic of the system is that it is at bottom paternalistic, indeed even feudalistic in spirit and motivation. (Feudalism ended in Japan only with the beginning of the Meiji era in 1868.) Most workers, both male and female, are recruited into the system on graduation, and while no contract to this effect is entered into, both parties understand that unless there is a specific contrary designation employment is for the duration of working life. Workers receive a starting wage on entry into a firm based on the level of education they have attained, and thereafter their base pay is determined mainly by seniority, with their earnings increasing each year in the firm until retirement. But in addition to this base salary, the firm will pay a great variety of benefits. These include housing — either in dormitories or company apartments — transportation, yearly or semiannual bonuses that may nearly equal the base pay, family allowances, insurance, subsidized midday meals, vacation facilities, athletic and recreational equipment, safety clothing, office uniforms, and medical services. In return, the worker, blue-collar or white-collar, expects to willingly perform a great deal of overtime work, to move willingly to various parts of the country as the company directs, to jealously guard company secrets, to resist pirating from other firms, and altogether to give the employer and his fellow workers his total loyalty. Chie Nakane, a leading Japanese anthropologist, depicts the institution to which an individual is attached as the chief factor determining his or her status. It provides the *ba*, the framework within which the individual finds a place. Furthermore, "Age and sex are superseded by status.... Age will become a deciding factor only among persons of similar status. Status also precedes sex. It is well known that Japanese women are nearly always ranked as inferiors; this is not because their sex is considered inferior, but because women seldom hold higher social status."[6]

These, at least, are the customs in the large firms — Sony, Hitachi, Toyota, Nissan, Japan Steel. But these large firms, influential and pattern setting as they are, employ only about 30 percent of the wage and salary earners, and an even smaller percentage of women. Perhaps 80 percent of women are employed in the medium and small firms, where about 70 percent of the total labor force works. And in this sector, the smaller the firm, the less binding the commitment to lifetime employment, the fewer the benefits and fringes, and the more

5

frequent bankruptcy, i.e., an absolute sundering of the employment relationship. It is not surprising then that in these firms there is a high rate of voluntary worker turnover, as the workers seek more secure, better paid employment within other small or medium firms and even occasionally, in periods of sudden expansion, in large enterprises.

The Japanese industrial system is usually described as a dual economy. The large firms represent the upper level with their modern equipment, their lifetime employment, at least of male workers, their high level of supplementary benefits, and their wage rates, which approach those of Western Europe and the United States. The medium and small firms are the underlayer. Here a majority of the workers have lower wages, less secure conditions, and few, low fringe benefits. In the upper level, hiring is of graduates with no — or very little — room for job-seeking adults; the lower level of the economy is more like a Western labor market with many adults changing jobs and looking for work in a market that offers, however, only limited opportunities.

In addition to full-time employment in the upper or lower levels of the economy, a third characteristic type of employment is what is called "temporary" or "casual" or "part-time." The large firms meet their needs for seasonal or other temporary expansion and hedge their manpower bets on the business cycle by hiring, in addition to their regular employees, short-term labor. Some of these workers may be furnished by contractors whose business it is to provide casuals and to pay and insure them from the contracted sums received from these large companies. Some are hired directly on contracts of usually short duration, two to six months. But these contracts are often renewed for years on end.[7] Most of these workers receive none of the lavish benefits and fringes given permanent workers, and they may work for years at an essentially unchanging rate of pay, even though they may work side by side, as many do, with permanent employees on the same assembly line or in the same office. Unions do not welcome temporary workers and rarely seek to organize them; indeed they usually exclude them from membership.

In spite of their high rate of labor market activity, women cannot be said to be really a part of the permanent employment system. To be sure, they start off at close to the same rate as men, but very quickly the gap between their earnings and those of men opens up and widens. Women are restricted to a narrow range of occupations, all considered auxiliary and, with a very few exceptions such as teaching, low-paid. Women are promoted much more slowly than men, when they move upward in skill or scope at all.

Even in government employment, the opportunities for work are not equal. Although recently the door was opened to admit women as maritime safety officials and air traffic controllers, there are still nine groups of occupations closed to women. The attitudes and practices with which women have to cope are well illustrated in a discussion one of the authors had with a group of women from a government tax office. Some quotations from this meeting illustrate the point:

Husbands often put wives under considerable pressure to quit work and remain at home because they think it does not look well for them if they permit their wives to work. . . .

In the tax office there is no clear policy on early retirement and no pressures from supervisors for women to retire. But when women have children they have to take more days off than men do and gradually they experience the feeling that they are taking advantage of their fellow workers and are regarded as failures within their group. This sense of their own inadequacy is bad for their work. . . .

Women do not yet have any clear sense of their right to work and therefore little feeling that they can or should defend their rights. . . .

Discrimination exists in a very fundamental form within the office. To obtain a job candidates must pass a national examination but there are two different examinations, one for men and one for women. The one for women admits them only to general office work; the one for men admits them to "tax work." As soon as they are hired, men are sent to school. Women start work without special training. Men are thus in the mainstream, women in subsidiary work. This division of assignments is based on the belief that women are not fitted for research or for inspection outside the tax office, that they can only work inside the office on routine assignments. Women are only very exceptionally promoted to work outside the office. . . .

The beginning wage for men and women differs, based on different work content. Men are promoted rapidly, women progress very slowly. As soon as men finish their six months of school, they get their first wage raise, women have to wait a year, though the civil service law provides only for annual increases. . . .

Men think of women as children, and this view is prevalent among male fellow workers.[8]

Women receive little or no on-the-job training. The employer does not expect them to remain with him more than a few years, for he and they understand the women will marry in their middle twenties, and when they do their main interest will presumably no longer be their work but their homes and their children. Because no employer expects them to do other than follow this pattern, he justifies giving them less training, and wants them to retire when they marry or have their first or second child, or when they reach the age of twenty-seven or thirty. This practice is euphemistically referred to as "early retirement." The employer genuflects in the direction of the established retirement system in that a woman "retiring" at this point receives a lump sum payment representing her acquired rights in the company's retirement system, which are based on the number of years she has worked. The employer may go further and collude with her to write her as unemployed so that she can draw unemployment insurance. That monthly income together with her lump sum payment constitute a kind of paternal dowry from the firm on the occasion of her marriage or the birth of her child.

As recently as ten or fifteen years ago, women "retiring" in this way usually did not return to the labor force unless they were widowed or their husbands became incapacitated. Now more than half of the women thirty to thirty-nine years of age and 64 percent of those between forty and forty-nine are working. In fact, the percentage of those working after forty is almost as high as that of women in the premarital years; in 1970 the actual numbers of older women working considerably exceeded the numbers of younger ones — an indication of the aging of the Japanese population as a whole.[9] It is also the trend that women are working more years now than they did just after the war. The Ministry of Labor's research on this matter shows that in 1960 the women working averaged 4.0 years of work life as compared with 7.8 for men, whereas in 1978 women averaged 6.1 years to men's 11.1, and the average age of working women had risen in the same period from 26.3 years to 34.1.[10]

But clearly, women returning to work after ten years or so absence from the labor market, are not reemployed in the upper level of the economy as "permanent" workers. By "retiring" they have given up all claims to returning to their former places of employment. A glance at the nature of their work and their location in the labor market shows that they are working in small companies or as unpaid family members or in the large companies as "temporary" or "part-time" workers at low wages, often uninsured and without fringe benefits or private pensions — certainly with no hope of promotion or improvement in their circumstances.

Most older women work part time. Officially this is defined as employment at less than thirty-five hours a week. Actually many part-time workers work full weeks and even overtime, since part-time status defines them not by the hours worked but as outside the regular labor force. A study done by the Tokyo District Labor Department in August 1974 on part-time workers found that at least one-third did some full-time work, and over 50 percent worked from six to eight hours a day. Only 32 percent were covered by health insurance and social security and 34 percent by unemployment compensation; 27 percent had paid vacations.[11] The Ministry of Labor in 1978 counted 2.15 million women working less than thirty-five hours a week, a 500 percent increase over 1965. The 1978 figures were a 5.8 percent increase over 1977.

This demand for part-time workers was at first a product of the shortage of labor in the boom years of the early 1970s when employers turned more and more to bringing women into the labor market on their own terms. Moriyama reports that of the 8.7 million women who have no jobs but are willing to work, 3.7 million or 40.8 percent want to work part time, a record high.[12]

A report of the Japanese government to the Organisation for Economic Cooperation and Development (OECD) in 1973 referred to this trend:

From the 1960s on, the shortage of young workers caused by rapid economic growth together with the changes in work performance due to technological innovation has led to an increasing demand for semi-skilled workers and people for monotonous or simple tasks. This has expanded employment opportunities and increased labour market mobility. Jobs have therefore opened up for older women, and to make full use of such women part-time work has been introduced on an increasing scale.[13]

Companies depend on turning out women before they have become expensive annual earners and replacing them with new graduates who will work for starting wages.

Nothing better illustrates women's unequal status than their wages. Although women's total cash earnings increased 16.1 times while men's rose 12.7 times between 1955 and 1978, women earned in 1978 56.2 percent of what men did.[14]

Starting wages for new graduates conform best, though still not very accurately, to the equal pay prescribed in the law. Up to age twenty there is not much difference in male and female earnings, but differences increase with age to peak between forty and forty-four. In 1965 women in the forty to forty-nine age group earned, in cash earnings, only 44.7 percent of men; by 1978, earnings had improved to 48.1 percent for ages forty to forty-four and to 50.6 percent for forty-five to forty-nine. By ages fifty to fifty-nine (after most male and all female retirement) the differential had moved from 46.0 percent to 52.1 percent for ages fifty to fifty-four, to 56.7 percent for fifty-five to fifty-nine, and to 68.9 percent for sixty to sixty-four. Women over age sixty-five earned 73.5 percent of men.[15]

Variations occur by industrial sector, though in every sector women receive far less on the average than men. In 1978, women in real estate earned 47.0 percent as much as men; in wholesale and retail trade, 50.6 percent; in the services 65.8 percent; and in transport and communications, 70.3 percent.[16]

In addition to all the other reasons employers give to justify these differences in pay, the fact is that the almost total segregation of occupations by sex means that men and women rarely do the same work. The consequence is that few opportunities arise to compare equal pay for equal or even comparable work.

Women and the Law

On the other hand, Japanese working women are the beneficiaries of considerable protective legislation, and in the view of many champions of women's rights, these acts are important because they are all the protection women have to compensate them for their many disadvantages and the generally discriminatory treatment they receive on the job.

These enactments are part of the Labor Standards Law and as such are enforced, or, better, enforceable by the Ministry of Labor's inspectorate, located in cities in each of the forty-six prefectures. In brief, the Labor Standards Law guarantees equal pay for equal work (Art. 4); prevents women from working during the hours from 10:00 p.m. to 5:00 a.m. (Art. 62); regulates the maximum amount of overtime allowed per day (2 hours), per week(6 hours), and per year (150 hours) (Art. 61); prohibits women from doing "dangerous work" — they may not work higher than five meters above ground nor lift specified heavy weights (Art. 63), nor may they work underground (Art. 64); they may request time off during menstruation when it interferes with their ability to work (Art. 67); they have a specified maternity leave of six weeks before and after childbirth, and the health insurance law (Art. 50, par. 2) provides for paying insured women workers 60 percent of their standard daily remuneration for six weeks before and after childbirth, if they should not work (Art. 50, par. 1). They may not be dismissed during maternity leave nor for thirty days after it (Art. 19). When a pregnant woman requires it, she may be placed on a lighter job (Art. 65). A woman may request time for nursing an infant under one year of age and receive at least thirty minutes twice a day during working hours (Art. 66).[17]

In 1972 the Diet adopted the Working Women's Welfare Law that aims to further the welfare and improve the status of working women by taking appropriate actions to help them reconcile their dual responsibilities of work and home or to enable them to develop and make use of their abilities.[18] Its adoption brought Japan closer to compliance with standards on women's employment laid down in the International Labour Organisation's (ILO) conventions on women's work. The law, however, was recommendatory, not mandatory, and left it to the women's bureau of the Ministry of Labor to endeavor to persuade employers to accept its standards voluntarily. In the years since the enactment of the law, the bureau, working through its prefectural offices, has been able to point to many examples of employers who have introduced some of the recommended reforms, but the law remains very much a statement of goals and intentions rather than of required conditions. Practical measures the law proposes to employers include provision "of any necessary child care facilities for the working women he employs, including the approval of child care leave (whereby women workers with babies or children are allowed, on request, to absent themselves for a fixed period to look after their offspring)" (Art. 11). The law also foresees improved vocational guidance and vocational training systems offered by state and local governments through welfare centers for working women, which will also offer "rest and recreation facilities."[19] Most prefectures and major cities have already established these centers. This law is perceived to be of major importance in enabling women to maintain their places "within the life-long employment and seniority wage system" by guaranteeing reentry to it after maternity leave and child care leave.[20] In 1975 additional legislation was enacted for child care leave that guarantees one year child care leave without pay to specified women workers.[21]

Conditions in public employment fall under a different set of laws that in some ways improve upon the provisions of the two laws noted above. Teachers in Tokyo, for example, have mandatory maternity leave eight weeks before and after childbirth with full pay, and a national law adopted in 1956 makes it mandatory that replacements be found for teachers taking maternity leave. Established because many women cut short their maternity leave because they know no substitutes are replacing them during their absence and their fellow workers are having to carry the load of their work, this regulation is an effort to ensure that teachers, at least, take full leave. Teachers may also take part of their prebirth leave when they experience morning sickness early in pregnancy, and public employees generally are allowed to come one hour late and leave one hour early during pregnancy in order to avoid rush hour traffic. Their nursing time is extended from the private sector's thirty minutes twice a day to forty minutes twice a day until the child is fifteen months of age.[22]

Nurses, however, many of whom work in public hospitals, are exempted from the ban on night work and are allowed to work eight nights a month. Actual circumstances are such, however, that, according to officials interviewed in the Japan Nurses' Association, few nurses have as few as eight nights a month on duty.

Menstrual leave is peculiar to Japan and two other Asian countries, Indonesia and Korea. Custom, as is often the case, antedates law. A study of its history shows that as early as 1927, Nihon Rōdōkumiai Hyōgikai, Japan's trade union conference, requested paid menstrual leave as one of its targets for general action. The first actual agreement was with Senju Food Institute in 1931. During World War II, it was widely introduced as a kind of reassurance to women entering the labor market, who were encouraged to do so in the face of the male labor shortage.[23] The law itself was agreed to by the American occupation authorities, who were apparently persuaded that the working conditions of Japanese women were particularly burdensome and toilet facilities in the postwar plants inadequate.[24]

The Japanese law allows for leave where "a woman suffers heavily from menstruation" or is employed on a job "injurious to menstruation." In such cases the woman requests leave from her employer. But the law says nothing about whether it is to be paid leave and in most cases it is not.[25] Although the law does not stipulate the length of such leave, collective agreements or work rules often call for up to two days per menstrual period. In 1976, 59.6 percent of companies provided that menstrual leave could be paid.[26]

Yet in 1978 only about 16 percent of women requested such leave. Apparently many hesitate to go to their employers with such a request. And indeed some women report that when they do, they are embarassed and harassed. One hospital, for instance, reads over the loudspeaker the names of women taking leave. Some say they cannot afford to take time without pay. In any case, among those requesting leave, the average number of times it was used was 6.7 per year, and the average number of days used totaled 8.4 in 1978.[27]

A paper prepared for the ILO by its Tokyo office on this subject points out that the employers' federation would like to delete all provisions concerning menstruation leave from the law, whereas the unions seem to concentrate mainly on the issue of whether it is to be paid or not. Dōmei, the right-wing socialist trade union federation, seeks one day's paid leave; Sōhyō, the left-wing federation, with organization mainly in the public sector, has apparently not included such a request in its proposals for reform. But among unions that have achieved contractual agreements for some or all of menstrual leave are a number affiliated with Sōhyō, including the telephone workers, (Zendentsū), the tobacco workers (Zen-senbai), and the postal workers (Zentei). Of unions affiliated with Dōmei, the textile union (Zensen) reports that 110 local unions in its organization have such provisions in their contracts; and a large local union of the electrical workers in the Oki Denki Corporation (affiliated with the independent federation Chūritsu Rōren) has won the first day of leave with full wage guaranteed and the second day with 80 percent of wages.[28]

On the employers' side, the contention is that women abuse the right to leave, taking it when they do not need it. Indeed, employers want to abolish it, pointing to the absence of such legislation in other countries and insisting that under modern hygienic conditions women do not need the leave. Some of the cases that women have taken to court, however, hang on these issues.

The employers' position has been supported to some degree, though for other reasons, in a recent action by the Labor Standards Law Research Society, an advisory body to the labor minister. It recommended that some of the existing protective measures for women in employment should be abolished in order to promote occupational equality of men and women.[29] The second subcommittee of the Labor Standards Law Research Society in its recent report on women's labor says that there is no medical ground for giving women workers menstrual leave and that the practice should be abolished. It suggests, however, caution in doing so, because the practice has been going on for the past thirty years, and therefore, "consideration should be given to the various circumstances involved in solving the problem.[30]

Despite all this attention to women in Japanese labor law, the code mentions sex equality only in respect to equal wages for work of equal value. The section of the law affecting conditions of work (Art. 3) speaks also of equality but limits it to creed, national origin, and social status, omitting sex. No mention is made anywhere in the law of equal opportunity in hiring, in training, in access to work or to promotion, although Article 14 of the constitution calls for equal rights of men and women before the law.

Whether Article 14 can be construed to cover contracts between individuals or private organizations is a matter of some debate among lawyers. Taken literally, the article applies only to contracts between the state and individuals. One scholar consulted believes that a majority of lawyers accept the narrow interpretation of the law. The opinion of a powerful minority, he says, is that the constitution is meant to have indirect as well as direct effect, and that the construction to be placed on Article 14 is that the constitution regulates public policy and is therefore concerned with private contracts. Moreover, the constitution speaks to the sanctity of contracts of all kinds and for the view that contracts must not violate public policy.[31]

Judges dealing with cases brought under Article 14 that involve women's labor contracts have, on the whole, been liberal in their judgments that the constitution is applicable only indirectly to such contracts but that women are entitled to equal treatment with men in respect to their working conditions. The outcomes of these cases and how the judicial mind has construed this point are discussed in detail later.

A paragraph in the Civil Code is also of importance. Article 90 requires that "good law and order are to be maintained." Lawyers bringing women's discrimination cases to the courts have in several instances appealed to this principle, and judges have frequently found that working agreements condoning disciminatory conditions for women are contrary to the intent and meaning of this article. This route is a clear way around the constitutional difficulty outlined above, since the civil law applies to individual and collective agreements and to a company's work rules.

Retirement Practices

An important issue in the cases on discrimination is the question of when women shall retire. Although women's years at work have increased considerably in the last decade, their work life remains much shorter than that of men.[32] A good deal of this extended work life is a product of the growing tendency on the part of women to return to work at middle age, but these women can rarely hope for permanent employment at this age and instead most frequently work as part-time or casual workers, meaning that they fall outside the private benefit system and not infrequently are unreported to the public system as well.[33] In addition, retirement at the end of a continuous work career may be not simply five years earlier than men but ten or more years earlier.

The notion that women should retire earlier than men is not, of course, peculiar to Japan. Many European countries, including most communist regimes, which vaunt their systems of equal rights for men and women, have laws calling for retirement of women five years earlier than men. Such laws tend, in cases where pensions are reckoned by years of employment and earnings, to put women to severe disadvantage. Where, as in East Germany and some other communist countries, pensions are paid on a flat monthly rate to all retired persons, women are no worse off than men, especially in view of the fact that pensions in these countries tend to be extremely low.

Pensions in Japan, as in many other countries, are of two kinds: a national social security monthly payment based on years of insurance to which the worker contributes throughout his or her working life and, particularly in the upper level of the economy, a sum paid by the firm. In Japan, this latter sum is usually based on years of work with the company, accumulated at the rate of about 2 percent of annual earnings per annum and paid as a lump sum on retirement. Under both systems, Japanese women suffer by reason of their low wages. But even more, when they must retire — not just five years but often as much as twenty-five years — earlier than men, they have little to fall back on. The lump sum they have accumulated by retirement from a firm, not as large as a pension, is treated as a kind of wedding or birth present and as such is a substantial "gift."

Most companies, including public ones, set a general retirement age at fifty-five. The unions have been urging, with some insistence, retirement at sixty and have succeeded in many companies in pushing the age upward toward that limit.[34] But wherever it is set, no one assumes that it will apply to the managers at the top or to the women at the bottom. And indeed men who are capable of continuing to work after fifty-five are usually reemployed after "retirement" for another four or five years, but at a lower salary than they received under the seniority system. The reason for early retirement is obviously rooted in the seniority wage system; it is a device for unloading older workers before they become unbearably expensive.

As for women, the authors have noted that often their employment contracts or the companies' agreements with the unions call for their retirement on marriage or at childbirth or not later than thirty years of age. Even when companies set older retirement ages for women, these limits usually fall five to ten years earlier than men's, and it is most unusual for a company to continue to employ a woman past her retirement, no matter what her age.

According to the report of the Labor Standards Law Research Society, 77.3 percent of the companies surveyed had a fixed retirement age for employees. Of these 23.1 percent were the same for men and women. Where retirement ages were different, in 99.7 percent of the cases men retired at ages above fifty-five and in 0.3 percent under fifty-four. For women, however, 3.5 percent retired at ages under forty, 54.9 percent between forty and fifty-five and 41.6 percent at ages above fifty-five. Special retirement conditions were reported in 7.4 percent of the companies for women. Of these, 88.1 percent required retirement at marriage (6.5 percent of the total), 35.3 percent had pregnancy and birth retirement requirements (2.6

percent of total), and 10 percent had women retire from the company at marriage to someone in the company (0.7 percent of total).[35]

The method of enforcement of the early retirement systems may be by work rule, by collective agreement, by individual contract with an employee, or, more usually, by customary practice. Table 1 shows the distribution by these categories.

TABLE 1

Enforcement of Retirement Systems
(% of firms surveyed)

Retirement Point	Work Rule	Collective Agreement	Individual Agreement	Customary Practice
Marriage	10.9%	1.0%	2.9%	80.9%
Childbirth or pregnancy	4.6	1.0	1.8	86.2
Early age	68.1	7.4	10.5	8.3
Nepotism	3.8		1.4	87.0

Source: Survey by Ministry of Labor, Women's and Minors' Bureau, 1971, as cited by Hayashi, "Litigating Tactics," pp. 2–3.

A distinctive point is the difference that in fact exists between companies' official retirement rules and the point at which it is "customary" for women to retire, earlier than the work rules or union agreements may call for. In such cases the company accomplishes its purpose by "hinting" to its woman employee at the appropriate time that she is no longer useful to the company and had better go. This disapproval by the employer is often supported in open and subtle ways by male and female fellow workers with the result that a protesting woman in the end cannot tolerate the loss of face involved in appearing unwanted every day for work and she agrees to early retirement.

A study by the Women's and Minors' Bureau of the Ministry of Labor in 1978 points to improvement in the ostensible discrimination against women in retirement policies (see table 2); however, the figures on the practices of women in firms designated as having customary uniform retirement tend to negate this impression (see table 3). It is important to note that in 1978 about three-fifths of the women who presumably have a customary right to the same retirement age as men in fact retired earlier than men.

TABLE 2

Uniformity and Inequality in Retirement
(in % of firms surveyed)

	Officially Uniform Retirement for Men and Women	Customary Uniform Retirement for Men and Women	Early Retirement for Women
1976	70.1%	23.5%	5.8%
1978	71.3	23.1	5.4

Source: Ministry of Labor, Women's and Minors' Bureau, *Shokuba ni Okeru Danjo Byodo o Susumemashō* [Let's implement equal working conditions between men and women], pamphlet no. 78, 1979, p. 6.

TABLE 3

Retirement Practices of Women
under Customary Uniform Retirement

	under 40	40 to 55	55 or higher
1976	5.6%	63.0%	30.3%
1978	3.5	54.9	41.6

Source: Ministry of Labor, Women's and Minors' Bureau, *Shokuba ni Okeru Danjo Byodo o Susumemashō* [Let's implement equal working conditions between men and women], pamphlet no. 78, 1979, p. 6.

Companies justify this special treatment of women on a number of grounds: that they have inferior physical power and intelligence and lesser commitment to work than do men; that married women have the burden of housework to carry and hence the energy that they can devote to paid work is diminished by this prior claim; that women do not justify companies' investment in their training because they have short working lives, which is particularly true of college graduates who come on to the labor market at twenty-two and leave at twenty-five or twenty-six to marry; that since women are not trained, they are not worth the higher levels of the seniority wage and the point at which their wage ceases to measure their usefulness is when the women reach their late twenties. Their jobs consist of so-called helping or supplementary work, and, so the employer position goes, they cannot be worth the same remuneration or consideration as men.[36]

As a consequence of this circular reasoning, women are not placed on promotional ladders. Of the companies surveyed by the Labor Standards Law Research Society, 47.7 percent offered chances of promotion for women while 52.3 percent did not. Among those employers who did not, 60.1 percent explained that "because women do supplementary work, it would be impossible," and 47.3 percent said "because women's overall employment time is so short."[37] Women are expected to remain in their original jobs as long as they work, receiving slightly higher increments each year of employment but fairly quickly reaching a ceiling above which it is not worth retaining them.

Notes

1. In 1978, 21.25 million women were in the labor force. This meant a participation rate of 47.4 percent. About 21.8 million were wage and salary earners and made up 33.0 percent of all paid employees. The remainder were self-employed or unpaid family members, mainly in small firms. Ministry of Labor, Women's and Minors' Bureau, *Fujin Rōdō no Jitsujō* [Facts on women's labor] (Tokyo: Finance Ministry Printing Office, 1979), pp. 1–2.

2. James Abegglen, *Japanese Factory* (New York: Free Press, 1958).

3. Among these have been Solomon Levine, *Industrial Relations in Postwar Japan* (Urbana: University of Illinois, 1958); Alice H. Cook, *An Introduction to Japanese Trade Unionism* (Ithaca: New York

Women in the Employment System

State School of Industrial and Labor Relations, Cornell University, 1966); Robert E. Cole, *Japanese Blue Collar: The Changing Tradition* (Berkeley: University of California Press, 1971); Kazuo Ōkōchi, et al., *Workers and Employers in Japan: The Japanese Employment Relations System* (Princeton: Princeton University Press, 1973); Kōji Taira, *Economic Development and Labor Markets in Japan* (New York: Columbia University Press, 1970); and M.Y. Yoshino, *Japan's Managerial System: Tradition and Innovation* (Cambridge: M.I.T. Press, 1978).

4. Robert M. Marsh and Hiroshi Nannari, *Modernization and the Japanese Factory* (Princeton: Princeton University Press, 1976).

5. Robert Dore, *British Factory–Japanese Factory: The Origins of National Diversity in Industrial Relations* (Berkeley: University of California Press, 1973).

6. Chie Nakane, *Japanese Society* (Berkeley and Los Angeles: University of California Press, 1970), p. 32.

7. See Mikio Sumiya, "Rinjiko Mondai no Genjō" [The present state of the issue of temporary employees], *Nihon Rōdō Kyōkai Zasshi* 5:3 (March 1963); and Katsumi Yakabe, *Labor Relations in Japan* (Tokyo: International Society for Educational Information, 1978), pp. 2–4.

8. This meeting took place in Tokyo, October 26, 1973. The *Japan Labor Bulletin*, April 1, 1980, reports, however, that the National Personnel Authority has swung open the door for women to qualify as national tax officers and "deliberations to permit women to take qualification examinations for this occupation from the next fiscal year have begun with the Tax Administration....These posts so far have been opened only to men....Of the 16 different qualification examinations for public employees implemented by the National Personnel Authority, the only occupations not yet accessible to women are prison officers and immigration guards."

30

9. Japan Institute of Labour, *Japan Labour Statistics,* (Tokyo: Japan Institute of Labour, 1974), pp. 40–41.

10. Japan, Ministry of Labor, Women's and Minors' Bureau, *Fujin Rōdō no Jitsujō* [Facts on women's labor] (Tokyo: Finance Ministry Printing Office, 1979), p. 54.

11. Cited in Yukiko Higuchi and Fukuko Sakamoto, eds., *Hataraku Fujin no Kenri to Tatakai* [The struggle for working women's rights] (Tokyo: Minshusha, August 25, 1976), pp. 54–58.

12. Mayumi Moriyama, "Women Workers in Japan," a paper prepared for the International Symposium on Women and Industrial Relations, Vienna, September 12–15, 1978; Moriyama is a former director of the Women's and Minors' Bureau, Ministry of Labor. Also, Ministry of Labor, *Fujin Rōdō no Jitsujō,* p. 59.

13. Organisation for Economic Cooperation and Development, "Manpower and Social Affairs Committee, the Role of Women in the Economy," *National Report, Japan,* processed (Paris: Organisation for Economic Cooperation and Development, September 13, 1973), p. 24.

14. Sangyo Rōdō Chōsasho, *Rōkihō Kaisei Mondai to Jyoshi Hogo Rōkihō Kenkyūkai Hōkoku ni Tsuite no Rōshi no Iken* [Issues on the revison of the Labor Standards Law and protection of women workers—the opinions of management and labor] (Tokyo: Sangyō Rōdō Chōsasho, 1979), p. 9.

15. Ibid. See also tables 11, 12, and 13 in Appendix A.

16. Ministry of Labor, Women's and Minors' Bureau, *The Status of Women in Japan* (Tokyo: Ministry of Labor, 1974), p. 18.

17. Ibid., pp. 20–21.

18. Ibid.

19. Ministry of Labor, "Working Women's Welfare Law," provisional translation, Law no. 13 of 1972 (Tokyo: Ministry of Labor, 1973).

20. U.S., Department of Labor, Employment Standards Administration, *The Role and Status of Women Workers in the United States and Japan — A Joint United States-Japan Study* (Washington, D.C.: Government Printing Office, 1976), p. 47.

21. Law Concerning Child Care Leave Granted Women Teachers in Compulsory Education Schools, etc., and Nurses, Dry Nurses, etc., in Medical and Social Welfare Facilities, etc., Law no. 62 of 1975.

22. National Personnel Authority Regulations 10-4, as cited in International Labour Organisation, "Health Protection of Women Workers" (Tokyo: International Labour Organisation [1973?]), p. 6.

23. Nobuyoshi Shimada, "Seirikyūka no Mukyūka Keikō to Seikyūken no Yōgo" [Trend of making menstrual leave unpaid and the case for the right to menstrual leave], *Rōdō Hōritsu Jumpō*, no. 860 (1974).

24. Interviews with Gail Nomura, University of Hawaii, and Professor Susan Pharr, University of Wisconsin, both doing research on the history of the American occupation policies in Japan immediately after World War II, early March 1979. Nomura supplied one of the authors with a document by Dr. Yutaka Moriyama, M.D., "Survey on Menstruation Leave," October 1948, which had, she believed, influenced the Americans' decision to include such a provision within the Labor Standards Law. The study shows that 80.3 percent of the women covered in the survey believed menstrual leave is necessary, with 42 percent believing that two

days' leave suffices, while 52.1 percent favored three days' leave. Nomura's research (not yet published) shows that such leave was first introduced in the textile industry before the war and became fairly widespread during the war when sanitary facilties were not readily available to women.

25. The National Personnel Authority (NPA), which regulates conditions in public employment, has listed jobs that are "injurious to menstruation" where leave may be sought, in contrast to those where "the measures decided by the NPA are taken in respect to those engaged in jobs not injurious to menstruation."

26. Ministry of Labor, *Fujin Rōdō no Jitsujō,* p. 147.

27. Ibid., p. 83.

28. International Labour Organisation, "Health Protection," p. 6.

29. Ministry of Labor, Women's and Minors' Bureau, *Fujin Rōdō Hōsei no Kadai to Hōkō — Rōkiken Hōkoku* [The problem and trend of the legal protection of women workers — report of the Labor Standards Law Research Society] (Tokyo: Nikkan Rōdō Thūshinsha, 1978), pp. 49–51.

30. *Japan Times,* November 28, 1978; Ministry of Labor, Women's and Minors' Bureau, *Fujin Rōdō Hōsei no Kadai to Hōkō,* p. 51.

31. Interview with Professor Tadashi Hanami, Dean, Sophia University Law Faculty, Tokyo, October 7, 1973.

32. See table 9 in Appendix A.

33. A prefectural director of the Women's and Minors' Bureau stated in an interview in 1973 that although women working part time legally should be covered both for workers' and unemployment compensation, many women in small industry are often not

enrolled. In her prefecture, 83 percent of women were in medium and small industry.

34. It is ironic that Japan, which has the lowest retirement age among modern countries, has in 1978 published longevity statistics showing that both Japanese men and women live longer on the average than persons in any other country. *Japan Labor Bulletin* (September 1, 1978).

35. Ministry of Labor, Women's and Minors' Bureau, *Fujin Rōdō Hōsei no Kadai to Hōkō,* p. 13.

36. This paragraph summarizes the authors' interviews with staff members of two departments of the employers' federation, Nikkeiren, held at various times at the organization's office in Tokyo.

37. Ministry of Labor, Women's and Minors' Bureau, *Fujin Rōdō Hōsei no Kadai to Hōkò,* p. 13.

2.
Cases on Discrimination

The Japanese are not a litigious people as compared with Westerners and certainly with Americans. Because their culture places high value on loyalty to their group and in employment the group is defined as their company, it is particularly difficult for an individual to break this constraint and charge an employer in open court that he has not been fair and loyal to his employee, the plaintiff. When grievances exist, Japanese are much more apt to seek out an individual mutually respected by the parties who will mediate their differences, thus saving face for each of the litigants and proposing a settlement each can accept. But since women are regarded as inferiors, it is difficult to mediate between a woman and a man. The go-between is not dealing with equals, and a settlement is hard to reach.

Whether for this or other reasons, the fact is that the number of women going to the courts with cases that charge discrimination in the workplace has greatly increased over the past few years. Enough of these cases have issued in settlements favorable to women to encourage more to take this route. A number of lawyers, particularly women lawyers, are now specializing in such cases,[1] and books recording case history have appeared in some numbers.[2]

Japanese Court System

The courts are organized in a three-tier pyramid: district courts, high courts, and the Supreme Court. There are 50 district courts, each with about 50 branches, 8 high courts with 6 branches, and a single bench in the Supreme Court, located in Tokyo.

Japan has both civil and criminal courts. With very few exceptions labor cases are judged by civil courts. A woman worker taking a case against her employer might well start her appeal at the Labor Standards Office, a section of the local branch of the Ministry of Labor. If the case had to do with wages, the Labor Standards Office inspector would have jurisdiction for an initial inspection. If the inspector found cause and could not settle the matter in conciliation proceedings with the employer, he or she could turn the case over to the public prosecutor for action in the courts.

Since the Labor Standards Law does not guarantee sex equality in respect to other issues — matters affecting marriage retirement or early retirement — in cases concerning these issues, the aggrieved woman must consult a private attorney and go to court on her own. Since the Japanese system does not rely on earlier court judgments as precedents, each judge is free to consult his or her own authorities and to deal with the issues and interpret the law according to his or her own lights. This applies to the courts at each level as well as to the individual courts and judges. The Supreme Court tends to be very conservative in dealing with labor cases, and decisions favorable to the complainant at lower levels may well be overturned when they reach the Supreme Court.

All discrimination cases begin in the district courts. In the usual cases, an employee challenging dismissal or compulsory retirement typically faces two kinds of proceedings. In the first she carries a provisional suit, asking the court to order the employer to continue the employee in her employment status until the end of the trial itself, because, she pleads, there is a strong possibility that she will win the case. At the same time she enters an original suit, asking the court to declare the employer's action null and void because it is against good public order or the constitutional guarantees or other provisions of the labor law. Miyo Nakamoto, whose case against the Nissan Automobile Company is discussed later, lost both her cases in provisional suits at the level of the district and high courts but won in the original suits at both levels.

The descriptions of cases in this chapter are arranged according to subject matter: equal pay, early retirement, transfer to distant localities, and problems related to maternity and menstrual leave.

Equal Pay

The equal pay cases rest on the presumable guarantee of equal pay in Article 4 of the Labor Standards Law. The article provides that "the employer shall not discriminate women against men concerning wages by reason of the worker being a woman."[3] The grounds for these cases involve any of at least three issues: equal pay for equal work, equal payment of fringe benefits, and the discriminatory effect of introducing so-called efficiency pay systems that reward workers differentially on the basis not of seniority but of ability. It is under efficiency pay systems that women's pay is invariably lowered since women are categorically presumed to have less ability and less commitment to work than men.

As mentioned earlier, few opportunities exist to compare equal pay for equal or comparable work. One exception, however, is in the banks where both men and women, at least in their early years of employment, work as tellers and clerks. It is not surprising therefore that the first case to go to the courts on equal pay was taken by women bank tellers.

This first case was in the Akita Sōgō Bank and came to court in 1975, twenty-eight years after the Labor Standards Law and its Article 4 on equal pay went into effect. The bank had established more or less equal pay scales for men and women up to age twenty-six, but at that point had introduced two different promotion rates for men and women, with the result that by age fifty, women were earning only about 60 percent as much as men of the same age. The court decided in favor of the women bringing the case, and that touched off a campaign among bank employees throughout Japan to insist that the Labor Inspectorate, charged with the enforcement of the Labor Standards Law, look particularly at wage scales in banks. The Labor Standards Office then directed its inspectors to examine the plants and offices they visited for wage scales as well as for health hazards and overtime violations. The inspectorate, in 1975, reported it had received some thirty complaints of violations of the equal pay provisions and to women in eight banks had ordered restitution amounting to more than one million dollars. But the problems in banks did not end with settlement of the equal pay cases. Other litigation with the banks is discussed elsewhere in this chapter.

A leading machinery company, Tōshiba Kikai Company, had been reprimanded in 1972 for having adopted with the union in the plant an agreement that set a ceiling on "age allowances" for women at twenty-two years of age, while men first reached their ceiling at forty-five. The woman carrying the complaint to her local labor standards office had first appealed to her union, only to find that it would give her no support because it was party to the agreement that locked her into the wage for twenty-two-year-olds, even though she had worked twenty-seven years for the company. The labor office reckoned that in 1970 and 1971 alone she had lost about $700. Some seventy-five women in the company had been treated in the same way and were presumably due similar amounts from the company. The company immediately consulted its head office in Tokyo, and at the time the case was reported in a national paper, it had not yet reached a decision. The chairman of the union pleaded ignorance of the law, and the news reporter concluded his article by stating that, "the recommendation of the Labor Standards

Office will have a delicate influence on the present struggle with the company for higher wages and the union leaders are in a difficult position."[4]

When the Nippon Shintaku Bank introduced a 4,000 yen monthly special allowance for its male employees, a female employee took her complaint to court. In this case the union supported its woman member. The matter was settled in September 1973 before the case came to trial after a woman Diet member raised a parliamentary inquiry into the matter, which resulted in the case being brought to the attention of the minister of labor. The publicity persuaded the company that it was in error.[5]

A woman employee of the Nissan Automobile Company has brought an equal pay case under Article 4 of the Labor Standards Law charging that she has been deprived of the family allowance paid by the company. Her husband is totally disabled, and she is head of household. The complaint went to the Labor Inspectorate, which recommended to the company in her favor. When she appeared at the payroll office to make her claim in person, she learned that the company's rules had changed so as to give the allowance to women only if they were widows or otherwise husbandless and supporting a family. The court had not yet acted on this case at the time of this study.[6]

A more subtle form of unequal pay results from

the introduction of payment by "ability" as an element in the traditional education-seniority pay system. Employers for years — to some extent in response to the prodding of Westerners who helped found, for example, the Japan Productivity Center — have announced they were introducing some relatively substantial element in the pay package that would represent ability. The degree to which this had actually occurred in most companies before the onset of the recession of the 1970s was probably not more than 15 percent of the total base wage. Since the recession, payment by ability has been added in many categories as a means of economizing on personnel costs. Women have suffered particularly, for their work is perceived to have a very low ability element, and the particular abilities women are believed to have receive low evaluations. (This practice and the discussion and assumptions underlying it are the Japanese equivalent of the job evaluation debate and its effect on women's work in Western Europe.) The cases on this issue have occurred in both public and private employment.

Kazuko Yamamoto, employed by Suzuka City, Mie Prefecture, in 1948, brought a case against the city in 1972 on the grounds that men doing office work in her department had both higher rank and salary than she who equaled or exceeded them in seniority. Twenty women in similar positions joined her in making her complaint that the city had set up a pay scale based on job evaluation. Promotional opportunities were attached to some positions; but women's jobs were all rated low, and the promotional possibilities hardly existed. Yamamoto charged that the city had established unequal pay scales for men and women. The employer responded that individuals differ in capacity and the differences in pay only reflected this element. The defense apparently did not attempt to explain why no woman's job required and no woman exhibited ability to meet the new measurements.[7] On February 21, 1980, this case was decided in favor of the plaintiff in Tsu District Court. But the public employer was not willing to accept the judgment. The *Japan Labor Bulletin,* April 1, 1980, reports that the case is on its way to the high court.

At the Shizuoka Bank, the distance between women's and men's pay widened rapidly after efficiency pay was introduced in 1966. Six women went to their union in 1973 to ask for help in dealing with the employer on the matter. The union, after several months, did take up the matter. As a result the bank gave women the same job titles as men but at one rank lower on the scale. For a time this certainly lessened the difference between them in pay, but it did not satisfy the women, who brought up their case repeatedly to the union. In October 1974, the group had grown to ten, and in June 1975 these ten women went to the local labor standards office to ask for an investigation and a recommendation to the company in their behalf. A woman Diet member, hearing of the matter, raised a parliamentary inquiry about the issue in the Social and Labor Committee, one of the standing committees in the lower house, and it in turn addressed an inquiry to the Ministry of Labor. The position of the ministry was that the bank had, after all, made an effort in the right direction in 1974 and that the complainants should be patient — and grateful — for these steps. The women's repeated efforts to animate the labor inspector to continue his activity were to no avail. The women have now turned to the courts where the case awaits hearing and judgment.[8]

Equal pay issues are comparatively straightforward since they are the subject of a section of the Labor Standards Law. Complaints can go without question to the Labor Inspectorate, which is set up to enforce all articles of the Labor Standards Law, with some hope at least of an examination of the facts in any specific case. The inspectorate, however, cannot itself prosecute and must turn over a recalcitrant case to the public prosecutor for court action. Records of the inspectorate up to 1975 showed that it had handled thirty cases on equal pay. How many of these were settled directly by the inspectors, and how many were turned over to the prosecutor is not clear. Hayashi comments that, "equal pay cases show that the legislation is only the beginning, and full implementation of this principle is still a distant target."[9]

Retirement Policies

Companies justify early retirement procedures by pointing out that women are for the most part doing "supplementary" work or work that does not need to be carried on further or work for which an inexperienced younger woman can readily be found. They contend that women contribute too little to the company to justify retaining them when their salaries under the seniority-education system must increase every year without accompanying increases in productivity. They point also to the protective legislation that requires them to give maternity leave when women become pregnant, and they note the other protections that must be accorded to pregnant women, all of which make them less efficient and more expensive to the company. Moreover, they believe that when a woman has a home, this becomes the primary focus of her interest and working efficiency necessarily drops.[10]

Retirement cases form the bulk of those coming to the courts alleging discrimination against women. They fall into five distinct categories, in each of which significant judgments have issued: retirement on marriage, retirement at childbirth, dismissal of "part-time" or "temporary" employees, retirement at age thirty, and different retirement ages for men and women at career's end.

On December 20, 1966, the Tokyo District Court judged unlawful a practice of compelling female employees to resign on marriage on the grounds that such action constitutes discrimination against women workers and is contrary to the freedom of marriage. The ruling, the first of its kind, upheld on appeal a case filed by Setsuko Suzuki, twenty-six years of age, against the mandatory dismissal by her employer, Sumitomo Cement Company, and ordered the employer to pay her 732,000 yen as the amount corresponding to her lost wages since her dismissal and to reinstate her in her former job as an office clerk of the company at the going rate of 22,975 yen monthly.

Suzuki, who during the period of her trial worked as a clerk in the company employees' union, began as a regular employee in July 1960 after signing a memorandum at the company's request to "resign voluntarily when she married or when she reached the age of thirty-five," as the company had adopted a plan of automatic retirement on marriage for its female employees. She married in December 1963, and in March 1964 the employer discharged her "for business reasons," referring to the memorandum she had signed. In October 1964, she sued the employer on the grounds that the dismissal was counter to the constitution and to the Labor Standards Law. She also charged that the memorandum should be voided since the work rules did not enumerate marriage as a reason for dismissal and that the request for such an agreement infringed her freedom of marriage. She pointed out that the union since May 1963 had been demanding the abolition of the early retirement system for women.

The company stated that in 1958 it had decided to employ female office workers as supplementary workers aiding male employees by copying, running errands, cleaning office rooms, or serving tea until their marriage. Under this system eighty-eight women had already voluntarily retired upon marriage. Thus the scheme was an established practice with the validity of a work rule.

The court found first that such a requirement of retirement on marriage constituted discrimination by sex, and this is explicitly forbidden under Article 14 and Article 24 of the constitution. Although the Labor Standards Law does not explicitly forbid discrimination by sex and allows reasonable distinction by sex in working conditions through the prescribed protective legislation, its basic principles forbid sex discrimination. Any collective agreement, work rule, or individual labor contract, the court said, that includes unreasonable discrimination by sex is null and void under Article 90 of the Civil Code, which provides for annulment of any act aimed at affecting matters in a way contrary to public policy and good morals.

In its decision the court directly denied that women's efficiency necessarily declines on marriage:

Under the present circumstances in this country, because of economic reasons, quite often there is a need for women workers to remain in employment even after their marriage in order to supplement their family income. Such female workers would have to seek other employment if they are discharged under the scheme of retirement on marriage. Due to the prevailing seniority-based wage system, employment opportunities for such married and middle-aged women are limited as compared with those for fresh school graduates. It is inevitable for them to reconcile themselves to lower employment conditions than those they hitherto enjoyed, even if they successfully obtain reemployment. Circumstances being such, the system of retirement on marriage forces female workers to choose between getting married and remaining in employment for economic reasons. Accordingly it may be reasonably said that the system in force limits freedom of selection of a spouse. Family is an important unit of society and an important part of the public order under law and should be respected as a part of the basic human rights.[11]

In the course of the decision, the court referred to Article 13 of the constitution, which protects an individual's right to life, freedom, and happiness, and to three other articles of the constitution: Article 24 guaranteeing equality and respect for the individual's home life, Article 25 protecting the individual's right to exist, and Article 27 covering the individual's right to work.[12]

Such a decision, if not appealed to the Supreme Court, would appear to have covered the ground and would in Anglo-Saxon law stand as a binding precedent, at least until another court had challenged its reasoning. Under Japanese practice, however, each case is applicable only to the plaintiffs at bar, and while judges hearing similar cases may cite — and in fact do cite — *Sumitomo Cement* as influencing their opinions, the decision has no further precedential power. In this case the company appealed indeed to the high court. The case, however, was settled before the court with the employee accepting the condition that she would retire after the birth of her second child. The system, as such, continued to exist.

Companies such as Ōita Broadcasting continue to publicly announce early retirement on marriage as a "gift from our company to the bride." Women, however, came to know the Sumitomo case and more and more widely made sport of the system, signing contracts calling for marriage retirement and then showing them to newspaper and television interviewers, counting on the resulting publicity to make it impossible for the companies to carry out their intent.

Seven cases in all have followed *Sumitomo,* among them *Hōkoku Industries, Kōbe Noda School,* and *Shigehara City.* In all of them the judges have found for the plaintiffs. Indeed all high courts now seem to be in agreement that forcing retirement for women at marriage is against "good order" as called for in Article 90 of the Civil Code.[13] In fact, the decisions are so clear and uniform that no new cases have been brought since 1973. Indeed the government is now considering taking the necessary legal or admonitory steps to require or advise the abolition of the system of retirement at marriage.[14]

A variation on forced retirement at marriage is dismissal of women in preference to men when a personnel cut is unavoidable. In *Furukawa Mining Company* a woman employee joined by five others charged that in the company reorganization women had been dismissed simply because they were married. The Supreme Court on December

15, 1977, held, however, that the plaintiffs were unable to prove that only married women were dismissed or that they were dismissed simply because they were married, and it ruled therefore that the dismissed plaintiffs had not necessarily been discriminated against.[15]

Kazumi Suenami was employed at the Ōsaka office of Mitsui Shipbuilding Company in March 1963 and continued to work there after she married in February 1968. In November of that year she applied for pregnancy leave. The company's response was to ask her to retire. She refused. The company insisted that it was entitled to deny renewal of her work contract after the birth of her first child "under an agreement concerning women workers." The agreement was one with the union that called for the retirement of all women at marriage. A proviso allowed some women to remain at their own request but on a year-to-year basis. With the birth of the first child, however, the contract would automatically cease to be in force.

In spite of the company's warning, Suenami returned to work after her maternity leave, and Mitsui Shipbuilding Company dismissed her on February 2, 1969. As its justification, management said that women workers, because they mainly attended to supplementary jobs such as filing and answering phone calls, must be treated differently from men as to their efficiency, which deteriorates markedly after marriage.

Presiding judge Chisato Ono of the Ōsaka District Court ruled on the constitutional question in Suenami's case, stating that the constitution governs only relations between individuals and the state and does not regulate such private contracts as hers with Mitsui Shipbuilding Company. He went on, however, to find that "the action of the Mitsui Shipbuilding Company was clearly unreasonable within the intent of the basic law and constituted an evasion of the intent of the Labor Standards Law." By the time Ono's decision came down, Suenami had had her second child and was successfully maintained in her claim of having a right to continue to work.[16] The company appealed to a higher court, but the authors have been unable to find a record of a decision on appeal.

A number of cases originating as dismissal because of childbirth are defended by the companies, as Mitsui Shipbuilding sought to do, on the grounds that the women plaintiffs are not permanent employees but part-time workers under limited contract. They are not therefore entitled implicitly or explicitly to job security in the lifetime system but may be let go with or without cause whenever a contract expires.

Atsuko Inoguchi was employed at the Sanwa Bank as a part-time worker on a one-year contract.

She did the same work and kept the same hours as regular, permanent employees from the time she started in March 1968. One year later she was dismissed because her contract had expired. She took the matter to court, but the Tokyo District Court ruled on December 20, 1973, against her. Although it said most temporary employment is for periods shorter than one year, usually two to three months, the fact that this contract was for one year did not give the employee any right to claim permanent employment. It was her obligation, the court advised, to find out at the beginning of employment what the duration of her contract would be. Since she apparently did not acquaint herself with these facts, she must bear the risk of not having her contract renewed.[17] On February 27, 1979, the Tokyo High Court ruled against her appeal.

At the Nagoya branch of Tōyō Seiki, six temporary workers who were on nine-to-five schedules — permanent workers were on duty from eight to four — were suddenly dismissed after three years' employment. Masako Tamaoki, one of the group, took her case of discharge to the Nagoya District Court. It decided that it was not the classification of the work that created temporary or permanent status but rather the nature and circumstances of the work. The court saw no reason for designating some workers part-time when they did exactly the same work for the same number of hours as full-time workers. The company has appealed the case to a high court.[18]

At the Tōshiba Yanagimachi plant, six temporary workers (one, a man) who had worked from one year to three years and eight months were laid off en bloc. The decision of the Yokohama District Court was in their favor on much the same grounds as in *Tōyō Seiki*. The case was appealed through the district court to the Tokyo High Court, and in each appeal the workers were sustained. The decision of July 22, 1974, held that "in cases like this, where a temporary contract has been automatically renewed a number of times, it is no different from a contract without limit," i.e., a permanent contract.[19] The mere expiration of a contract in such a case is insufficient for dismissal when no substantive reason for separation is offered.

A third dismissal of a part-time worker occurred with an art student working as a waitress in the Shumpū-dō department store restaurant. She was dismissed at the end of a year ostensibly because her boss did not trust her. When her efforts to get the store workers' union to help her were of no avail, she took the case to the Tokyo District Court charging unfair dismissal. Under examination her employer admitted that he had no real reason for letting her go. In a decision rendered December 19, 1967, the court held that an employee who has worked a full year can no longer be considered just a part-timer but a "worker with a contract for an undetermined length of time."[20]

Thus the so-called part-time or temporary workers on renewable contracts would appear to have won substantial consideration as permanent workers, providing sufficient time has passed to allow for the satisfactory completion of what could be seen as a probationary or test period.[21] Even so, the degree to which women placed on similar contracts following marriage can then be dismissed at any time later, whether because of childbirth or advancing age, appears still open. It is worth noting that the Labor Standards Law permits dismissal only for cause, and although it almost surely was written to refer to cases of permanent and not temporary or part-time employment, the judges' ruling in *Tōyō Seiki* and *Tōshiba Yanagimachi Plant* that an often-renewed temporary contract constitutes a permanent obligation is a significant judicial step.

At Nissan-kōki (the case is referred to by the company's earlier name, Tokkū Kikan Kōgyō), men and women had had the same retirement age of fifty-five until 1966. In that year, however, the company signed a contract with the union calling

55

for women to retire at age thirty. As early as 1963 the company had introduced a "job level evaluation system" that defined all women's work as "light, supplementary" work. By this designation women's wages were automatically set at the lowest point on the scale and presumably justifiably below those of all men.[22] A protest followed, so effective that the company reversed its decision and substituted for it a proposal, to which the union also agreed, that all women retire twenty-five years earlier than men, i.e., at thirty. On April 1, 1967, all women over thirty were dismissed. One of the women affected, Suiko Shiga, brought the matter to court and in so doing found herself a nationallly known figure, heading a national movement of women similarly dealt with in other companies. Support organizations sprang up all over the country, and their assistance enabled her to carry the case through to a favorable decision on July 1, 1969. The company's appeals, all of which were lost, delayed her return to work until March 1972 when her reinstatement became unavoidable. It occurred, however, as the result not of a judicial edict but of an agreement with the union before the court that the company extend women's retirement age from thirty to fifty.[23] This five-year difference between women's and men's retirement age is, as mentioned earlier, widely customary.

In the early 1970s, a similar issue arose in *Nagoya Broadcasting Company,* which was decided in 1974 in favor of the three women involved. In both this and *Tokkyū Kikan Kōgyō* the courts have pointed out that early retirement is not prohibited by the Labor Standards Law, but that such a wide difference in age at retirement between men and women is unreasonable discrimination against women and hence against good public order as called for in Article 90 of the Civil Code.

In two earlier cases involving the broadcasting company two women who had protested their dismissal at thirty had been admonished by the court for not bringing their cases before they were dismissed when the court could have issued a stay. It had pointed out that it had no power to reinstate them after the fact. Thus in this case, Mutsuko Shimizu and Katsuyo Oki, as they neared their thirtieth birthdays, instituted proceedings before dismissal, and the court moved to stay the company's hand. Then Yoko Narazaki of the Tokyo branch office brought her case on the same issue. The company's defense before the court, as presented by a vice president, was that at thirty women lose their beauty and ability. Michiko Tanaka, MP, as she has done in other cases, raised a parliamentary inquiry to the minister of labor using this quotation and calling for the revocation of the broadcasting company's license on the grounds that it had violated its obligation to promote political neutrality and good order.[24] This episode no doubt contributed to the wide attention given the case and may account for the company's having reinstated the women. In any case, they not only regained their jobs but got six years' back pay to cover the long period of the legal proceedings.

The company, however, has since ceased to employ women except on one-year contracts. An inquiry made in 1980 supplied the information that the company now has about forty part-time women employees and only eight full-time women employees. The reason for the union's failure to act in this matter can be found in the fact that labor relations policy in Japan commonly accepts that hiring and job assignment are company prerogatives over which the union does not endeavor to exert control.

Thus, although the court's action solved the problems of the three women, no court, in all probability, will extend aid to women under recruitment for part-time positions, so described, nor under the terms the company will henceforth offer its female recruits.[25]

Custom in Japan has laid down an unusually early standard retirement for workers, fifty-five to sixty years of age. Practice further specifies that women shall retire five to ten years earlier than men. Two cases, however, in both of which the Supreme Court appears to have spoken definitively, would seem to have corrected this differential where a company officially states its retirement age.

The first of these was *Izu Cactus Park,* where, under conditions of public employment, men retired at fifty-seven years of age and women at forty-seven. Five women employees, Kuni Hara, Sueko Hiyoshi, Fumiyo Ishii, Sadako Ishii, and Natsuko Okamoto, claimed before the court that this was a violation of the equal treatment provisions of the constitution and of the intent of the Labor Standards Law. Countering their claim, the public employer argued that (1) tourist business requires youthfulness among female staff; (2) women's work ability is inferior to men's; (3) women age faster than men; and (4) the seniority-age wage system would require that women be paid very high wages for what are essentially supplementary jobs.

The case went to the Supreme Court on August 29, 1975. It rejected all these arguments and held that the early retirement system, while it does not violate any explicit requirement of the Labor Standards Law, is against the Civil Code's demand for "good public order."[26]

Izu Cactus Park represented a major victory for women who saw such differential retirement ages as discriminatory, but in most industry and public jobs the difference in retirement for men and women is not ten but five years. It is exactly this issue that has been before the courts for over ten years in the next case.

Nissan Automobile Company is extremely complicated, for it contains a long history of Miyo Nakamoto's employment, dating back to her resistance to dismissal at the end of World War II when a predecessor company sought to retire all its women war workers. Over the years, her employer has been at least twice absorbed in mergers by other companies, and these changes in ownership brought with them changes in company rules and in labor relations with different unions. All these events, however, are at play in the current case or cases, for in fact Nakamoto has had to ask the courts to clarify her employment status as well as her right to equity in retirement. The former issue was finally decided in her favor in 1973; the latter is now before the Supreme Court. Aside from Nakamoto's remarkable tenacity in pursuing her rights over thirty years, the case illustrates a number of significant points about Japanese law and custom in respect to the issue of retirement.

The immediate predecessor company to Nissan Automobile, Prince Automobile, where Nakamoto was employed, had no differential retirement age, and the union of which she was a member had a contract with the company to that effect. On merger with Nissan, the majority of the Prince union joined a rival union in the Nissan company. She, however, remained with what was a minority union and claimed that its contract had continuous effect. The Nissan Company's retirement agreement with the majority union specified retirement at fifty-five for men and fifty for women. Nakamoto was terminated in 1969 when she turned fifty, but she continued the case. In the meantime Nissan raised its retirement age in 1973 for men to sixty and for women to fifty-five. Accordingly, Nakamoto changed her claim for equal treatment to conform to the new male standard.

During its many years before the courts, the case became a topic for national discussion, for it challenges a concept accepted not only in Japan but in many industrial countries, namely, that women as they approach retirement are less productive than men. The case was particularly notable, however, because of the arguments before the courts and the opinion of a lower court judge.

The Tokyo District Court on April 8, 1971, and the Tokyo High Court on March 12, 1973, ruled against Nakamoto in the provisional suit on the basis that a study published by the government purported to show that women's ability at fifty-five is comparable to men's at seventy.[27] But, only eleven days later, the Tokyo District Court ruled in the original suit that the five-year difference in retirement age between men and women was opposed to the Civil Code's requirement for "good public order."[28] The company appealed to the high court, and the high court ruled in favor of Nakamoto on March 12, 1979, just in time to save the case from becoming moot on the plaintiff's sixtieth birthday. Immediately a company announcement carried the word that, on demand of the union, the retirement age for women would be raised from fifty-five to sixty, effective April 1, 1979.[29] At the same time the company entered an appeal from the decision to the Supreme Court.

Nakamoto called the authors' attention to a second case pending against Nissan Automobile Company by a woman asking for damages amounting to her loss of salary for the five-year difference in retirement age. The court had reviewed her argument, but deferred dealing with her case until the Nakamoto matter reached decision.

The issue is still not definitively settled and may elude judicial determination for some considerable time, particularly if companies follow the Nissan pattern of reaching agreement with their unions in time to meet a plaintiff's demand but before judgments can issue, or indeed of keeping the matter in court until the plaintiff's age makes the issue moot.

Transfer

When women endeavor to resist company regulations or customary practices that would force their early retirement, companies sometimes respond by making their life on the job so difficult that the women give up the struggle and accept dismissal, or "retirement." For example, persons who refuse to accept transfers to inconvenient or distant places — and transfer is often a form of discipline imposed on these women — are guilty of disobeying supervisors' orders and thus make themselves liable to disciplinary dismissal. The court then has to decide whether the transfer was unfair punishment or whether it was indeed necessitated by conditions of the business. Discriminatory transfers affecting women are essentially of three kinds: those that separate married couples; those that are meant to be punitive because of union activity; and those that are meant to discourage married women from continuing to work.

A married woman school teacher and civil servant reported that when she turned forty her supervisor told her she was no longer useful to the school. She was at the time the mother of a school-age child and had taken some days off to care for the child when he was ill, thus inconveniencing school operations to some extent. The supervisor, at first "hinted" to her, as the Japanese say, that she ought to resign voluntarily. When she did not, she was transferred to an island in the Tokyo school district that had transportation back to the mainland she could use only on weekends. She admitted defeat and gave up the effort to continue in her profession, although she was a public employee and presumably especially protected in her right to equal job opportunity.[30]

A second type of transfer used to discourage married women is that imposed after a woman returns from maternity leave. It is a variation of dismissal imposed for childbirth.

At Tōyō Kōhan, Shūko Tachinaka had worked in the office and been active in union affairs. In April 1969, in the midst of her maternity leave, she received a notice that she would be transferred to become a cook for the male employees' dormitory. She refused to accept the assignment and received notice of dismissal. Within this same year, almost all newly married women were being dismissed, and two new female employees signed agreements that they would leave voluntarily on marriage. The few who were not dismissed on marriage were let go at the birth of their first child. Tachinaka herself had been "encouraged" to retire when she married with the statement from her supervisor that "a woman should retire when she marries; being in the home will make her happiest." When she became active in union affairs, her husband was transferred from Yokohama to Kyoto, but two years later he was returned to his post in Yokohama. Again, when Mrs. Tachinaka requested maternity leave she was urged to quit, and when she turned down the proposal she was told she "had no job to come back to." When she received her notice of transfer to a position as dormitory cook, it is not surprising that it was with the justification that with a child she was "only half a person.[31] When she refused to accept the transfer she was fired and went to the Yokohama District Court. Its ruling in the provisional suit on August 24, 1972, called for her reinstatement, a judgment that was overruled by the Tokyo High Court on October 28, 1974. On February 8, 1980, Tachinaka and her employer reconciled before the court, and she began to work April 1, 1980.

As in the case of the woman schoool teacher, discriminatory transfer to separate married couples may be used to punish one or both members of a couple for a misdemeanor or for recalcitrance to company orders or for union activity.

In 1966 a couple named Kazuko and Teruo Ogihara complained to the Akita District Court that the bank that employed them wished to send them to separate locations, that this would seriously disrupt their marriage, and that they therefore asked the court to stay the transfer order. The company pleaded that place of work was part of work content and that if the worker could not fulfill this important aspect of the job, he or she was of no use to the company. In this case business necessity required the transfers. The plaintiffs replied that the necessity of change in location must be balanced against the well-being of the worker who may be separated not only from spouse but from children by such a transfer.

By 1967, thirteen couples who had been separated by transfers of this kind formed a national organization to protect the right of couples to live and move together, and by November 1971, when they held their ninth meeting there were sixty couples in the organization. They appeal to Article 752 of the Civil Code, which prescribes that couples "must live together and equally help each other."

The courts in these cases have balanced business necessity against worker welfare and divided about fifty-fifty in their decisions. In *Ogihara,* the Akita District Court came down on the side of worker welfare on July 30, 1968.

The first case involving transfer meant to be punitive because of union activity came to the Chiba District Court in December 1960. In *Tsukamoto General Industries,* the company was charged with having transferred one spouse on the grounds that he was engaged in undesirable union activities. Since union activities are protected under the Trade Union Act, the company was ordered to reinstate the man in his former position on December 16, 1960.

These cases give the courts little trouble because not only does the Trade Union Act in Article 7, Section 1, make it unfair for an employer to penalize a worker for union activities, but the constitution guarantees in Article 27 the right to work. Some judges in dealing with these cases have found such transfers also not in line with Article 90 of the Civil Code protecting good civil order. Employers have several times been told by the courts that they must use their right to transfer "responsibly."[32]

Maternity and Menstrual Leave

Although the law calls for maternity and menstrual leave for women, women who try to take full advantage of these types of leave frequently find themselves additionally discriminated against. They may be asked to take retirement or be transferred to other less desirable jobs as a result of exercising these rights. Substitutes for women on leave are rarely available, with the result that women know their absence represents additional burdens to their fellow workers.

The problem is that the rights laid down for women during pregnancy and menstruation rest on the women's notification of their employers and on asking for the considerations which the law provides. No real provision is made to implement these rights. "The degree to which the law is used is therefore fractional at best," said Professor Susumu Satō of Japan Women's University, a well-known authority on the social security and labor laws. "For instance, when pregnant women ask for lighter work, one has to remember that most women work in medium and small businesses where the owner may genuinely not be able to make work lighter and cannot therefore accommodate his pregnant employee." Professor Satō went on, "One has to remember that sense of rights is not yet sufficiently developed either among employers or among women themselves that a request is easy for a woman to make or compelling upon her employer. In most cases, women simply give up. Either they go on working at the risk of miscarriage, or they quit work and lose both the right to legal leave and any guarantees of being able to return to work after childbirth. In the case of pregnancy where the woman does not get lighter work and continues to insist upon it, an employer is apt simply to say, 'Why don't you leave?'"

Professor Satō pointed out additionally that both ILO Conventions 102 and 103 guaranteeing these rights during pregnancy are under only reluctant consideration by the government, because changes in the direction of conformity with these conventions would cost both government and the employers considerable sums, which they are not willing to pay unless woman power is absolutely essential in their labor market.[33]

Maternity leave is paid at 60 percent of standard salary from the health insurance funds and is therefore not a direct cost to the employer. Menstrual leave is not required to be paid (with those occasional exceptions where unions have bargained for paid leave), so that absence from work is at the woman's expense, and while most women feel that menstrual leave is necessary, many cannot afford it and do not take it. In 1978 the Ministry of Labor reported only 16 percent of women employees took menstrual leave and that this percentage has steadily decreased every year since 1965.[34]

The cases arising therefore have to do with discriminatory transfers or retirement of women during or immediately after taking maternity leave and with employers creating a variety of difficulties for women who request menstrual leave, steadfastly refusing to institute payment for such leave and even unilaterally refusing to continue paid leave they have negotiated with the union.

Although there are eighty-four working days (twelve weeks) a year for which maternity leave might be sought, a study by the Women's and Minors' Bureau in 1974 showed the following use of maternity leave by the women surveyed: 5.3 percent took one to seven days leave; 12.0 percent took eight to twenty-one days leave; 19.7 percent took twenty-two to thirty-five days leave; 36.5 percent took thirty-six to forty-two days leave; and 23.3 took more than six weeks leave. Thus, about 74 percent of the women took half or less of their legally prescribed leave.[35]

In the early 1970s, Professor Satō surveyed a random sample of women in the medium-size city of Kanazawa. He asked a total of 372 working mothers how they had handled pregnancy and work and learned that 108 had worked continuously through to childbirth; 86 retired on marriage or pregnancy; 8 retired at pregnancy and returned to work when the child was seven months old; 31 retired in the first half of pregnancy; 22 retired in the last half of pregnancy; 21 retired after childbirth; 7 worked until the child was one year of age; 7 worked up to the sixth month of the child's life; 5 worked up to childbirth, retired for six months, and then returned to work; 12 started work only after marriage or childbirth; and 30 gave up work before pregnancy.[36]

According to a Ministry of Labor study in 1978, 36.7 percent of pregnant women or women who had given birth to a child retired. This percentage was highest in the big companies with more than five hundred employees, 40.9 percent.[37]

Shūko Tachinaka's case at Tōyō Kōhan challenged this kind of discriminatory action.[38] Her company said plainly that having given birth, she was only "half a person." Although her case was upheld, the Tokyo High Court in its judgment included the following caution, one which might well give any woman concern about adjustments and countermeasures to which she would have to accommodate herself on her return to work from maternity leave. The court said,

Needless to say a mother is protected for up to one year after giving birth and this protection under the law must be assured. ... At the same time, these women must consider that such provisions put certain demands on the employers.... The indication is that work efficiency is lowered and hence it is only reasonable to permit employers to take measures which will balance this effect in the workplace in their treatment of other workers.[39]

Among unions that have negotiated paid leave for women during menstrual leave, some have had to defend or fight again to maintain paid leave that employers have decided unilaterally to abandon.

Nurses at the Keiō University Hospital in Tokyo had for a time under union contract received two days of leave with pay. Early in 1970 the hospital unilaterally refused to continue paying for menstrual leave, and in 1973, after considerable unsatisfactory negotiation, the nurses took their case to court, hoping to restore the operation of the contractual clause. After long delays but before the case had been called, the parties in 1977 were able to negotiate a settlement out of court in which the hospital agreed to pay for one day's leave instead of the two the nurses had previously had a right to. The collective agreement covering all hospital workers now includes this provision. Since the settlement, 30 to 40 percent of the women use the leave, a somewhat higher number than did so during the years when it was not paid.[40]

The Teikoku Kōshin-jo Company in 1973 was paying one day's menstrual leave per month when the women in the company's employ asked the Nagoya District Court to require that the company pay for the two days which they allowed. First the district court ruled against the women on February 26, 1971, and then the Nagoya High Court on October 15, 1973. Similarly, a year later, May 27, 1974, the Tokyo District Court heard a case against the NBC Kōgyō Company brought by its women employees. On the grounds that the company paid a bonus only to workers who had no absentee records, the company, they said, had cut off bonus payments to women taking menstrual leave. The women claimed the leave was a right and taking it should not make them guilty of absenteeism. The court upheld the company's policy and denied the women's claim.

These women appealed the decision to the Tokyo High Court, arguing that the company does not penalize persons for taking leaves for marriages or funerals and it should not for menstrual leave. They noted that the work rules of the company contain no reference to menstrual leave, although it is part of the law; this omission was condemned as early as 1974 by the director of the Women's and Minors' Bureau of the Ministry of Labor, but her dicta have no power and apparently little influence.[41] On March 19, 1980, the Tokyo High Court upheld the decision of the lower court.

A worker at Teikoku Kōshin-jo in Nagoya had her menstrual periods every twenty-eight days and thus from time to time had two periods within the same calendar month, in which case the company refused her leave. The court to which she took her case defined the law to mean lunar not calendar month and sustained her contention that she was entitled to leave at each period.[42]

At Zenkin Takeda in Tokyo the collective agreement called for twenty-four days of menstrual leave a year with full pay. The company unilaterally promulgated a work rule that changed this payment to 68 percent of normal wages, and the Tokyo District Court on November 21, 1976, sustained the company because these women, it ruled, do clerical work for which a 68 percent payment is reasonable, since the number taking leave is low and full payment for this minority would constitute an inequality favoring the absentees over those who work full time. The Tokyo High Court decided in favor of the employees on December 20, 1979.[43]

The courts for various reasons find little ground for supporting menstrual leave with pay. The unions are modest in their programmatic demands on this point, and the vast majority of local unions that do the collective bargaining have taken no position on the matter of paid leave. Employers would like to do away with the right to leave altogether and have announced their determination not to pay for leave. Feminists and labor union women, government policy makers and legislators are somewhat at odds on supporting the need for leave as an integral part of the struggle for equal rights for Japanese women. On the one hand, a lawyer pleading many of these cases has said,

"There is no inconsistency between this legislation and the drive for equality. Men and women are different physically. Menstruation is a preparation for maternity, and women need the assurance of health and safe conditions for themselves and their offspring."[44] The unions similarly are unwilling to modify a gain which to them seems well and hard won.

On the other hand, the influential staff in the Prime Minister's Office that was set up after International Women's Year for the planning and promotion of policies relating to women in Japan has issued a plan of action that asks "the government to review the special statutory protective measures for women in order to determine the rational scope of protective legislation for women and to abolish such measures as prove to be scientifically groundless and impede equality between men and women in employment."[45] Since the chief piece of protective legislation under debate is menstrual leave, there can be little doubt as to how this item of the plan is meant to be interpreted.[46]

In view of these differences in approach and the growing though still small group of militant feminists agitating for changes in Japan comparable to those in Western industrial countries, it is timely to ask what the future holds for Japanese working women.

Cases on Discrimination

Notes

1. Among these lawyers are several consulted in preparing material for this book.

2. In addition to the books referred to in following footnotes are special issues of *Jurist,* a leading legal journal, several articles in leading national and provincial newspapers, and the following studies: Nobuyoshi Shimada, *Hataraku Fujin no Kenri Tokuhon* [Book of rights of working women] (Tokyo: Rōdō Jumpōsha, 1975); Nihon Koku Kempō, *Byodoken* [Right of equality] (Tokyo: Sanseido, 1977); Fujin Rōdō Mondai Kenkyūkai (Study Group on Working Women's Problems), *Gendai no Fujin Rōdō Mondai* [The problems of present-day working women] (Tokyo: Rōdō Jumpōsha, 1975); Ryōko Akamatsu, ed., *Nihon Fujin Mondai Shiryōshūsei* [Collection of materials on Japanese women's problems], vol. 3, labor (Tokyo: Domesu Shuppan, 1977); Saburō Matsuoka, *Fujin Nenshō Rōdō* [Women and minors' labor] (Tokyo: Sōgō Rōdō Kenkyūsho, 1979); and Sangyo Rōdō Chōsasho, *Rōkiho Kaisei Mondai to Jyoshi Hogo — Rōkiho Kenkyūkai Hōkoku ni Tsuite no Rōshi no Iken* [Issues on the revision of the Labor Standards Law and protection of women labor — the opinions of labor and management] (Tokyo: Sangyo Rōdō Chōsasho, 1979).

3. The wording of the law as translated leaves it unclear whether its authors had in mind a distinction between "equal pay for equal work" and "equal pay for work of equal (or comparable) value." The cases that have so far been won suggest only the former. Ministry of Labor, Women's and Minors' Bureau, *Status of Women in Japan* (Tokyo: Ministry of Labor, 1974), p. 19.

4. *Asahi Shinbun,* April 8, 1972.

5. Hiroko Hayashi, "The Litigating Tactics by Working Women: Coping with the Gap between Legal Norm and Social Norm,"

paper prepared for the International Sociological Congress, section on women's movements, Uppsala, Sweden, August 13, 1978, p. 4.

6. Interview with Miyo Nakamoto, Tokyo, March 5, 1978. For information on Nakamoto's own case against the same company involving other issues, see p. 60.

7. Yukiko Higuchi and Fukuko Sakamoto, *Hataraku Fujin no Kenri to Tatakai* [The struggle for working women's rights] (Tokyo: Minshusha, 1978), p. 107; and interview with attorney Masako Ōwaki, Tokyo, March 3, 1978.

8. Higuchi and Sakamoto, *Hataraku Fujin no Kenri to Tatakai*, pp. 108–9.

9. Hayashi, "Litigating Tactics," p.4.

10. Higuchi and Sakamoto, *Hataraku Fujin no Kenri to Tatakai*, pp. 120–22.

11. *Sumitomo Cement,* December 20, 1966. *Rōminshu* 17, 6:1418.

12. Ibid.: 1419.

13. Interview with Professor Yoshito Yamamoto, Tokyo, March 1, 1978.

14. Interview with Hisako Takahashi, then director of the Women's Section of the Women's and Minors' Bureau and now director of the bureau. Ministry of Labor, Tokyo, February 21, 1978.

15. *Furukawa Mining Industry Co., Rodo Horitsu Jumpo,* no. 952 (1978), p. 81.

Cases on Discrimination

16. *Japan Times,* December 11, 1971.

17. Higuchi and Sakamoto, *Hataraku Fujin no Kenri to Tatakai,* pp. 68–69.

18. Ibid., pp. 69–70.

19. *Tōshiba Yanagimachi Plant, Hanrei Jihō,* no. 752 (1974), p. 28.

20. Higuchi and Sakamoto, *Hataraku Fujin no Kenri to Tatakai,* p. 67.

21. Ministry of Labor, *Rōdō Haskusho* [White paper on labor] (Tokyo: Nihon Rōdō Kyokai, 1979), pp. 208–9.

22. Ryōko Akamatsu, ed., *Joshi Rōdō Hanrei* [Decisions on women workers] (Tokyo: Gakuyoshobo, 1976), pp. 16–17.

23. Higuchi and Sakamoto, *Hataraku Fujin no Kenri to Tatakai,* pp. 132–33.

24. Interview with Michiko Tanaka, MP, House of Representatives, March 7, 1978.

25. Interview with Masako Ōwaki, lawyer of the plaintiffs in this case, Tokyo, March 3, 1978. Two of the women in the case have since left their jobs voluntarily. As of 1980, only Katsuyo Ōki is still employed at Nagoya Broadcasting Company.

26. *Izu Cactus Park,* February 26, 1975, *Rōdō Hanrei,* no. 319 (1975).

27. According to Nakamoto, the study was based on materials gathered by the Ministry of Agriculture and Forestry in a single remote mountain village of Akita Prefecture in 1953. It was an area where early death was unusually frequent, and it was this fact and not the conditions of industrial factory or office work that were

being studied. Nonetheless, as late as 1977 the argument also convinced a judge in *Nisseki Karatsu Hospital.* Efforts on the part of Nakamoto's defense group to have the Women's and Minors' Bureau of the Ministry of Labor have the study withdrawn from current circulation were unsuccessful, she reported. Interview with Miyo Nakamoto, Tokyo, March 5, 1978.

28. For a full discussion of the case, see Masako Ōwaki, "Nissan Jidōsha Sabetsu Teinensei Hanketsu no Igi to Mondaiten" [The meaning of the decison on discrimination on retirement age in the Nissan Automobile industry] , *Jurist* 695 (1979): 77 ff.

29. *Japan Labor Bulletin* 18, 8 (August 1979): 2.

30. That government as an employer often lags instead of leads is illustrated in one statistic concerning women technical and managerial workers. In nongovernment employment 8.8 percent of this category is female, whereas in the civil service only 0.9 percent of managerial posts are held by women. Japan, Prime Minister's Office, *Population Census, 1975,* as cited by Moriyama, "Women Workers in Japan," p. 13.

31. Higuchi and Sakamoto, *Hataraku Fujin no Kenri to Tatakai,* pp. 157–60.

32. Ibid., pp. 152–53.

33. Interview, Tokyo, October 1, 1973.

34. Ministry of Labor, Women's and Minors' Bureau, *Fujin Rōdō no Jitsujō* [Facts on women's labor] (Tokyo: Finance Ministry Printing Office, 1979), p. 83.

35. Ministry of Labor, Women's and Minors' Bureau, *Fujin no Ayumi 30 Nen* [Thirty years' women's progress] (Tokyo: Rōdō Horei Kyokai, 1975), p. 264.

Cases on Discrimination

36. Interview with Professor Susumu Satō, October 1, 1973.

37. Ministry of Labor, *Fujin Rōdō no Jitsujō,* p. 83.

38. *Tōyō Kōhan,* Yokohama District Court, August 24, 1972, *Rōdō Hanrei,* no. 162 (1973); Tokyo High Court, October 28, 1974, *Rōdō Hanrei,* no. 213 (1975).

39. Quoted by Masako Ōwaki, "Maternity Protection as an Excuse for Discrimination," *Feminist* 6 (1978).

40. Interview with Fukuko Sakamoto, lawyer for the nurses, Tokyo, March 23, 1978.

41. Higuchi and Sakamoto, *Hataraku Fujin no Kenri to Tatakai,* p. 196.

42. *Teikoku Kōshin-jo,* Tokyo District Court, October 5, 1973, *Rōdō Hanrei,* no. 191 (1974).

43. *Zenkin Takeda,* Tokyo District Court, November 12, 1976, *Rōdō Hanrei,* no. 264 (1977); Tokyo High Court, December 20, 1979, *Rōdō Hanri,* no. 332 (1980).

44. Interview with Fukuko Sakamoto, Tokyo, March 23, 1978.

45. Japan, Prime Minister's Office, Commission for the Planning and Promotion of Policies Relating to Women in Japan, *National Plan of Action* (tentative translation) (Tokyo: Prime Minister's Office, January 1977), p. 9.

46. On this point, the report of the second subcommittee of the Labor Standards Law Research Society reads: "Laws protecting 'motherhood' must be carefully considered and can be necessary, but for limitations outside of 'motherhood' protection we must reconsider the necessity of them and if they are contributing to

Cases on Discrimination

discrimination. In general, then, we feel that safety laws must be basically the same for men and women and as for employment limitations for women, they must be limited to laws necessary for the physical and various functional differences between men and women (considering the motherhood factor). ... Protective law must be limited to matters that have real reasons — there are at present protective laws that no longer have any scientific basis and become a hindrance to working women." Ministry of Labor, Women's and Minors' Bureau, *Fujin Rōdō Hosei no Kadaito Hōkō*, pp. 41–42.

3.
What Lies Ahead?

Action toward improving conditions of women is going ahead along at least three lines: (1) issues of harassment, downgrading, equal job opportunity, and job assignment are still being brought before the courts; (2) the Socialist Party, the Democratic Socialist Party, and the Communist Party have each presented a bill that would provide equal job opportunity similar to that provided by the British and United States antidiscrimination and equal job opportunity laws; (3) the staff of the planning and policy commission in the Prime Minister's Office issues studies of women's present status[1] and initiates programs that both voluntary organizations and government bureaus are urged to implement. The government has undertaken a number of programs to implement the recommendations of the Labor Standards Law Research Society.

To the extent that litigation has become a way out of discrimination for Japanese working women, it will continue to be used and is worthy of note, by persons outside Japan as well as inside, as a gauge of the degree and nature of women's discontent and exploitation.

That litigation has been as successful as it has is largely the result of the work of a small but dedicated group of women lawyers, several of whom we interviewed. But since cases take a very long time to run their course through Japanese courts, no successes would be possible without the support groups that gather round to raise money, inform Diet members who can then raise parliamentary inquiries that may move the Ministry of Labor or other government bodies into action, and provide publicity. For this latter purpose, an equally dedicated group of women journalists have succeeded — sometimes against editorial odds — in keeping the issues before the reading and listening publics. That these support groups are often allied with the radical parties is not surprising, though that fact is to some extent a deterring and divisive factor in gaining broadly based support in some cases.

On the whole, the unions have not been active in these cases. Their indifference is a product of a variety of factors. First, union contracts are never written for units larger than the single firm and very often for the single plant or branch (only in the public corporations are they national in scope). The national federation, and often the national union, has no power or influence over the content of these contracts and only rarely has a record of what their contents are. Hence many contracts are written in agreement with the company's discriminatory policy, and no national body is in a position to impose sanctions or discipline, even if it would.

Second, union leaders by and large share the societal views about women at work. They believe that women are and should be only transitorily in the labor market and that as short-term or part-time workers their concerns are of secondary importance to those of the genuinely lifetime male employees.

Third, reliance in determining conditions of work and particularly of women's work rests largely on law and less on collective bargaining.

Fourth, almost no women are visible in union leadership, even in those unions with large female memberships, such as workers in textiles, telecommunications, government service, teaching or department stores. Again, this is in part a product of women's short average work lives, but it is unquestionably a product of the low regard and low status that women have in the world of work. Every union and union federation has, to be sure, a women's division, and women are often active and effective shop stewards, but the women's divisions have little standing within the union executive bodies. While their recommendations may be listened to and even occasionally given rhetorical support, women are not part of the decision-making bodies of the unions.

Fifth, union women in even nominal positions of leadership, such as heads of the women's division, are torn between supporting programs launched from the outside by feminist groups or government bodies and supporting the position of the union that they represent.

Change is perhaps suggested if not clearly forecast: in 1980 both Nikkyōso, the teachers' union, and the Socialist Party have a woman as vice president. Moreover Sogyororen (Commercial Workers' Union) adopted at its 1979 convention a resolution seeking by fiscal 1980 the extension of the retirement age for all employees, regardless of sex, to age fifty-five, with the option for employees to continue working to age sixty at their request, and by 1985, a further mandatory extension to age sixty with optional reemployment to age sixty-five. The *Japan Labor Bulletin,* April 1, 1980, termed the proposal a "positive move towards the abolishment of the gap in mandatory retirement ages between male and female workers."

The existing legislation has its limitations. Although many aspects of women's work life are protected in the present labor code, the question of equal job opportunity is totally absent, and cases whose issues go to this point must be raised in constitutional or Civil Code terms that are extremely general. The courts, by and large, have found favorably against early retirement and most recently against differential retirement ages for men and women. The issue on which the women unionists are at present most determined, namely, retention of the right to menstrual leave, if possible with pay, will rest apparently much more on the unions' ability to bargain for such leave as a right with or without reimbursement. Indeed, very powerful forces, including agencies represented in the advisory commission to the prime minister are advocating serious reconsideration and probable abolition of this protection. The Women's and Minors' Bureau of the Ministry of Labor is probably, after some indecision, going to follow the lead of the advisory committee's action plan. Of great influence was the report of the Labor Standards Law Research Society. Following its suggestion that a new law to promote equal opportunity and treatment be enacted and that guidelines covering the handling of discrimination cases aid both the public and the government in putting the law into practice, the Ministry of Labor in 1979 established a committee on the study of equality for the sexes to work out the necessary guidelines. Fifteen members from management, labor, and the public have been appointed. Nine of them are women.

The issue of equal job opportunity has, however, hardly been addressed. Women's work roles are so secondary to men's in status, quality, length of service, training, and training opportunities that the question of equality in this sphere has hardly been realistically discussed. Yet the worldwide information and the growing number of personal contacts that International Women's Year made possible on a continuing basis have appealed to many leading women in Japan with the result that three parties have now each introduced a bill on equal opportunity. These efforts indicate how the Japanese are working with models provided by the British antidiscrimination law and the United States' Equal Employment Opportunity Act. The first was the JSP bill sponsored by Sumiko Tanaka, Socialist deputy in the House of Councillors. Within one or two years, there will be a bill by the government. The authors talked with Sumiko Tanaka frequently over a number of years, observing the way in which ideas on this subject took form in her drafts of legislation and discussing with her the strategies she hopes will bring her bill into law "within a ten-year period." She has prepared a bill to "promote equality of treatment for men and women in employment."

The bill would prohibit employers and other institutions from discriminative treatment against women and establish an equal employment commission to relieve women of such discriminative treatment by providing "a prompt and proper procedure in case of their allegation."

On the first point, the JSP bill reads in part: "Employers shall not discriminate against women on grounds of sex in respect of working conditions, concerning recruitment or appointment, wages, promotion, age limitation, retirement"; it further prohibits discriminatory treatment in employment exchanges and vocational training institutions and programs. The Central Equal Employment Commission is directed to enumerate in guidelines definitions of discriminatory treatment.

The commission would have a central body of national scope with subsidiary commissions in each prefecture. Each commission would be tripartite, representing employers, workers, and the public: "More than half the members of each group must be women." Women workers could complain first to their local commission with the right of appeal to the central commission. The commissions would hold open hearings, find fact where that procedure might be reasonable, and at their discretion order such measures as reinstatement, back pay, and other forms of relief to women workers determined to have suffered discrimination.

Law suits could be instituted against decisions of the central commission before the Tokyo High Court.

The central commission would also be authorized to advise the labor minister on measures "to be taken to promote equal treatment for men and women in employment."[2]

Tanaka assured the authors that "by the time the Women's Decade ends, Japan will have equality legislation...." It is even possible that the ruling Conservative party (LDP) will come forward with its own bill on equal opportunity and antidiscrimination in order not to have to deal with a bill on this subject that has been put forward by the Socialist Party.

The report of the Labor Standards Law Research Society represents the strongest and most influential statement that can be made for a reevaluation of Japan's present protective legislation for women in contrast to laws based on more equal treatment of the sexes. That, together with the recommendations of the Advisory Commission on Planning and Promotion of Policies Relating to Women established during the International

Women's Year in the office of the prime minister suggest undercurrents so powerful that the government is likely within a relatively short time to respond.

In January 1977 the commission, made up of representatives from the major women's organizations including both the left- and right-wing unions, together with women in management, issued its *National Plan of Action*.[3] The section on working women calls for:

Improvement of the employment systems and practices so that men and women can have equality of opportunities and treatment in all the spheres of occupational life

The government to review the special statutory protective measures for women in order to determine the rational scope of protective legislation for women and to abolish such measures as prove to be scientifically groundless and impede equality between men and women in employment

The government to encourage employers to adjust the conditions of working environments so as to more widely utilize women's ability

The government to conduct necessary guidance to improve the working conditions and the personnel management of part-time workers.[4]

By November 1977 the government had announced a priority plan for implementing the National Plan of Action by 1980. Point five of the eleven points of the priority program calls for sex equality in employment.[5]

What Lies Ahead?

What is largely lacking as a propulsive force to push government initiatives more rapidly along is a massive women's movement such as exists in a number of Western countries. A dedicated corps of women lawyers, journalists, academics, legislators, and public servants raise the issues and publicize them. A number of outraged women carry cases to court independently and are supported by ad hoc groups of supporters who raise the money to pay their costs and to sustain them, often through years of litigation. The national unions and their federations, which might supply the mass base, the money, the power, and the momentum to attack problems, not only on behalf of disadvantaged individuals but of women categorically, are unable and even unwilling to act concertedly on these issues.

Working women in Japan will at best make slow progress toward equality. The amazing thing is that they keep at it and that on at least some of their issues, the courts find in their behalf.

Notes

1. A recent study, sponsored by the commission, on women's participation in decision-making in both public and private sectors states: "Findings indicate that only 2.3 percent of all those who held managerial positions beyond the level of section chief were

women who were supposed to be qualified to participate in decision-making at their organizations." *Japan Labor Bulletin* 18, 8:2.

2. Interview with Sumiko Tanaka, House of Councillors, Tokyo, March 2, 1978; also letter from Tanaka to Alice H. Cook, June 5, 1978, enclosing a document entitled "The Purpose of the Bill Concerning Promotion of Equality of Treatment for Men and Women in Employment," May 11, 1978.

3. The commission's staff directors have been drawn from the top women in the ministries. The first two moved quickly from the commission into important diplomatic posts: Manae Kubota is presently assistant director of the Advancement of Women Branch of the Center for Development and Humanitarian Affairs at the United Nations in Vienna, while Ryōko Akamatsu in September 1979 became minister of Japan to the United Nations. The third staff director is the former head of the Women's Division of the Women's and Minors' Bureau of the Ministry of Labor, Hisako Takahashi, and the fourth, Tomoko Shibata.

4. Prime Minister's Office, *National Plan of Action*, pp. 9–10.

5. *Japanese Women*, March 1, 1978 (Tokyo: Fusen Kaikan).

Appendix A:
Women in the
Japanese Labor Force

The tables that follow describe women's position in Japan's labor force over a period of the fifteen to twenty years prior to 1974; in most cases it has been possible to update these figures to 1978. Most of the tables are taken from a publication of the Women's and Minors' Bureau of Japan's Ministry of Labor, *Fujin Rōdō no Jitsūjo* [Facts on women's labor] (Tokyo: Finance Ministry Printing Office, 1979). The source notes indicate where that is not the case.

Table 1 shows that women make up a little more than half the population age fifteen and older, the potential labor force. Of Japan's 53 million persons in 1974, women totaled 20 million. By 1977 their numbers had grown to 21 million.[1] In 1974 women made up then 37.3 percent (by 1978 about 38.4 percent) of the entire labor force. Women's labor force participation rate is 46.5 percent (by 1978, 47.4 percent) as compared with 81.8 percent for men (by 1978, 80.3 percent).

Table 2 shows labor force participation rates by sex and age. The figures show that while men's participation rate was expected to hold above 96.2 percent for the important twenty-five-to-fifty-four-year age groups throughout the seven-year period, women's rate was expected to drop even more sharply in the years after marriage (about age twenty-five) through the whole range.

A comparison of women employees by age group between 1960 and 1978, table 3, shows where the shifts in labor force participation are occurring. Women are staying in school longer and hence the participation rate of the group fifteen to nineteen years old has fallen almost 16.4 points. The group aged twenty to twenty-four, most of whose members are customarily single, holds fairly steady across the period from 1970 to 1978, while the group of women in their early years of marriage who are working has risen by more than 6.0 percentage points. And so, for each successive cohort up to and beyond retirement age, participation rates are significantly higher for each group.

Table 4 illustrates how the women in the labor force are distributed among self-employed, unpaid family workers, and paid employees, and a second distribution shows how they appear in the nonagricultural sector of the labor force. In the first, 13.8 percent were self-employed and 24.6 percent were unpaid family workers. Thus, nearly 40 percent of all women are not receiving wages or salaries; in the nonagricultural labor force, the number of nonemployees falls to about 30 percent. It is of considerable interest however that women have moved steadily into paid employment over the twenty years shown here. The number of self-employed in both distributions has grown by almost 20,000, but women in paid employment have risen from 7 to 12 million. Thus of the employed labor force, women make up 33.7 percent.

Table 5 reports on women in nine industrial categories. When compared with men's numbers and participation rates, women are, as in other countries, grouped heavily in three or four of the sectors. Their heaviest representation is in manufacturing, with 29.8 percent; followed by wholesale and retail trade, finance, insurance, and real estate, which account for 31.5 percent; and the services, with 27.7 percent. These rates have changed over the twenty-year period reported here. Men's employment is more widely spread among the nine categories: 28.9 percent of all men are in manufacturing; 21.4 percent are in wholesale and retail trade, finance, insurance, and real estate; 14.8 percent in the services; 13.9 percent in construction (where only 4.1 percent of the women work); and 12.5 percent in transportation, communication, electricity, gas, and water supply (where 3.1 percent of women are employed). In government, 6.4 percent of the men are working but only 2.7 percent of the women.

The greatest changes within any industrial sector have occurred in manufacturing where about twenty years ago 36.4 percent of women employees were working and only 32.5 percent of the men. Women have moved significantly into wholesale and retail trade — in 1978 about 250 percent as many were employed in this sector as in 1960, and men's employment in this sector also increased something over 200 percent. Mining and agriculture are declining in employment for both men and women. In 1960, 5.0 percent of women worked in agriculture and forestry, and only 3.5 percent of all men. By 1978 only 0.7 percent of women and 0.8 percent of men were in this area. Fisheries and aquaculture have faced comparable employment losses, as has mining, but the proportions of men in these occupations continue to exceed those of women by a small amount.

Most women are at work in medium and small industry, and table 6 shows the percentage of women in the industrial categories of this size industry, usually defined as between

95

Appendix

fifty and five hundred employees. In 1970 women made up 62.6 percent of all workers in textiles in these enterprises, 71.0 percent in apparel, 43.3 percent in electronics, and 40.7 percent in precision machines, with only a slightly lower percentage in rubber. The proportion of women has risen most rapidly over the ten years reported here in furniture and fixtures, leather, transportation equipment, and precision machines.

Table 7 shows changes in women's occupational status. Over the eighteen years covered by the table, women have gained 14.1 percentage points in their proportion of both employees in the professional and technical category and clerical workers, with small gains among managers and officials and workers in transport. Moriyama noted in her paper at the Vienna Symposium that

the ratio of women in managerial and decision making posts, which normally require a certain length of time to reach, is 5.6 percent of all women workers. The number is small, but the increase has been remarkable being 2.4 times in the last ten years.[2]

They have lost most noticeably in their proportion of farmers (10.4 points) and among sales workers and service workers (3.2 and 3.1 points respectively).

Table 8 shows the proportion of married to single women in employment. A decisive shift has taken place over the sixteen years covered in the table, with the proportion of married women in paid employment almost doubling over this time.

Table 9 shows that over twenty-four years women's average age in employment has risen from 25.4 years to 34.1, an increase that is largely the product of the increasing number of married women in the work force. The average number of years of work for women has risen from 3.6 to 6.1. Men's working lives have also lengthened, and their average age in employment increased, but not nearly in such a decided way as women's.

Table 10 deals with part-time work. As might be expected, women make up the bulk of persons working less than thirty-five hours a week, over 60 percent of these workers. Their participation in part-time work has increased from 8.9 percent to 17.2 percent. Men's part-time work has decreased over the same period from 5.2 percent to 4.7 percent. Women's rate of increase is about 200 percent as compared with men's decrease of about 10 percent. Even so, women working less than thirty-five hours a week make up only 5.8 percent of Japan's nonagricultural employees and thus represent a smaller percentage of women's work force and of total labor force employment than in many Western countries. (About one-third of Sweden's women are working part time, and the proportion is slightly higher in the United States.)

Turning now to earnings, table 11 shows that women's incomes in relation to men's have improved somewhat in the 23 recorded years, both in terms of contractual or base rates and of special cash earnings. Nevertheless, the differential between men's and women's earnings in Japan remains far wider than in most industrialized countries, where women now usually earn 60 to 85 percent of men.[3]

Table 12 makes clear that men's and women's starting rates are not very far apart. Table 13, however, shows that the differentials widen with advancing age. Again, it is possible to say that women's rates relative to men's have improved over time, but the gap is very great. The slight percentage decrease in the differential after age fifty-five is due to the fact that in these years both men and women return to work after retirement and are employed typically on short-term contracts as "temporary" or casual workers, who for the most part receive no fringe benefits in cash from their employers.

The evidence is clear that the trend for married women to work is progressive and has reached a high proportion of the female labor force. Moriyama cites a study done by the Women's and Minors' Bureau in 1971 that revealed that in only 14 percent of the establishments surveyed were all women single; in the remaining 86 percent, married women were employed. She goes on to call attention to the fact that in the same year 10 percent of all women workers were reentrants after a period of interruption of work. These women returned to the labor market at an average age of thirty-two; 70 percent of them were married and 80 percent of the married women had children, the youngest of whom was on the average 8.6 years old. Thus for reentrants, the "retirement" from work lasts only about six years, takes place after the birth of the first or second child, and, once the child is launched in school, the mother returns to the market for employment. Moriyama attributes the tendency to remain at work — or alternatively to reenter at a fairly young age — to the increase in part-time work and the rise in women's educational level. This latter particularly has the effect of keeping women in the higher professions and in technical employment at work after marriage.[4] The steadily growing inflation undoubtedly accounts for women in less interesting and rewarding jobs continuing to work after marriage.

The differential between men's and women's earnings in Japan is very wide; relatively few women engage in part-time work; women are heavily represented in about four of the nine or ten industrial sectors and appear very sparsely in the others. These general observations can be made in a number of other countries but in respect to each, Japanese women are at the lower extreme.

Notes

1. Corrections to 1977 may be found in Mayumi Moriyama, "Women Workers in Japan," paper prepared for the International Symposium on Women and Industrial Relations, Vienna, September 12–15, 1978.

2. Ibid., p. 14.

3. Women in production work in Sweden are now earning 88 percent as much as men. Women in the United States have received between 61 and 63 percent of men's earnings over the period from 1967 to 1976. U.S., Department of Labor, Bureau of Labor Standards, *U.S. Working Women: A Data Book* (Washington, D.C.: Government Printing Office, 1977), p.34.

4. Moriyama, "Women Workers," pp. 12–13.

TABLE 1

Population and Labor Force of Women

(x 10,000 persons)

	1960	1965	1970	1975	1978
Total					
Population age 15 and over	6,520	7,287	7,885	8,443	8,726
Labor force	4,511	4,787	5,153	5,323	5,532
Women					
Population age 15 and over	3,370	3,758	4,060	4,344	4,487
Labor force	1,838	1,903	2,024	1,987	2,125

Source: Prime Minister's Office, *Labor Force Survey*, cited in Ministry of Labor, *Fujin Rōdō no Jitsujō*, p. 35.

TABLE 2

Labor Force and Labor Force Participation, by Sex and Age

	Total	15–19	20–24	25–29	30–34	35–39	40–54	55–64	65+
Women									
Labor Force (x 10,000 persons)									
1973	2,047	113	350	212	210	238	639	211	77
1974	1,999	95	319	217	210	229	645	209	75
1975	1,987	85	301	226	204	227	654	215	76
1978	2,125	79	273	242	227	255	720	240	89
Labor Force Participation (percentage)									
1973	48.2	28.0	67.3	44.4	46.9	56.1	61.3	44.3	16.7
1974	46.5	23.9	65.9	43.3	44.9	54.7	60.3	43.4	15.7
1975	45.7	21.7	66.2	42.6	43.9	54.0	59.9	43.5	15.3
1978	47.4	20.2	68.3	46.6	47.6	57.2	62.0	45.5	15.8
Men									
Labor Force (x 10,000 persons)									
1973	3,279	105	413	465	439	417	935	342	166
1974	3,311	97	378	489	458	412	971	341	168
1975	3,336	83	351	521	454	412	1,002	344	169
1978	3,406	74	293	502	469	437	1,104	353	175
Labor Force Participation (percentage)									
1973	82.1	25.2	79.9	97.7	98.4	98.1	97.3	86.5	46.6
1974	81.8	23.6	77.9	97.2	98.3	98.1	97.3	86.1	45.7
1975	81.4	20.5	76.5	97.2	98.1	98.1	97.1	85.8	44.4
1978	80.3	18.1	71.6	96.2	97.7	98.0	96.9	85.3	41.5

Source: Prime Minister's Office, *Labor Force Survey*, cited in Ministry of Labor, *Fujin Rōdō no Jitsujō*, pp. 36–37.

TABLE 3

Women Employees by Age
(x 10,000 persons)

Age	Number			Participation Rate			
	1960	1970	1978	1960	1970	1978
Total	738	1,096	1,280	21.9%	27.0%	28.5%
15–19	157	138	73	35.1	30.3	18.7
20–24	265	317	243	39.3	59.8	60.8
25–29		124	173		27.1	33.3
30–34	116	89	133	17.3	21.3	27.9
35–39		106	145		21.0	32.5
40–54	127	252	394	19.0	26.5	33.9
55–64		59	97		13.6	18.4
65 and older	5	12	23	0.7	3.0	8.1

Source: Prime Minister's Office, *Labor Force Survey*, Ministry of Labor, *Fujin Rōdō no Jitsujō*, pp. 52–53.

Note: Participation rate is percentage of paid employees in population 15 years old and older.

TABLE 4

Distribution of the Labor Force by Employment Status
(x 10,000 persons)

	Total		Self-employed		Family Worker		Employed	
All Industry								
Women								
1960	1,807	(100.0)	285	(15.8)	784	(43.4)	738	(40.8)
1965	1,878	(100.0)	273	(14.5)	692	(36.8)	913	(48.6)
1970	2,003	(100.0)	285	(14.2)	619	(30.9)	1,096	(54.7)
1975	1,953	(100.0)	280	(14.3)	501	(25.7)	1,167	(59.8)
1978	2,083	(100.0)	287	(13.8)	512	(24.6)	1,280	(61.4)
Men								
1960	2,629	(100.0)	721	(27.4)	277	(10.5)	1,632	(62.1)
1965	2,852	(100.0)	666	(23.4)	223	(7.8)	1,963	(68.8)
1970	3,091	(100.0)	692	(22.4)	186	(6.0)	2,210	(71.5)
1975	3,270	(100.0)	658	(20.1)	127	(3.9)	2,479	(75.8)
1978	3,325	(100.0)	677	(20.4)	124	(3.7)	2,519	(75.8)

103

TABLE 4 — *Continued*

		Nonagricultural Industry					
	Total		Self-employed		Family Worker		Employed
Women							
1960	1,146 (100.0)		200 (17.5)		245 (21.4)		701 (61.1)
1965	1,325 (100.0)		195 (14.7)		237 (17.9)		893 (67.4)
1970	1,561 (100.0)		208 (13.3)		264 (16.9)		1,086 (69.6)
1975	1,630 (100.0)		201 (12.3)		267 (16.4)		1,159 (71.1)
1978	1,781 (100.0)		221 (12.4)		286 (16.1)		1,271 (71.4)
Men							
1960	2,018 (100.0)		350 (17.3)		93 (4.6)		1,575 (78.0)
1965	2,359 (100.0)		350 (14.8)		85 (3.6)		1,924 (81.6)
1970	2,690 (100.0)		406 (15.1)		90 (3.4)		2,191 (81.5)
1975	2,975 (100.0)		435 (14.6)		75 (2.5)		2,458 (82.6)
1978	3,038 (100.0)		461 (15.2)		73 (2.4)		2,498 (82.2)

Source: Prime Minister's Office, *Labor Force Survey*, cited in Ministry of Labor, *Fujin Rōdō no Jitsujō*, pp. 40–41.

Note: Figures in parentheses are percentages.

TABLE 5

Number of Employees and Percentage Distribution, by Sex and Industry
(x 10,000 persons)

	1960	1965	1970	1975	1978
Total					
Total employees	2,370 (100.0)	2,876 (100.0)	3,306 (100.0)	3,646 (100.0)	3,799 (100.0)
Women	738 (100.0)	913 (100.0)	1,096 (100.0)	1,167 (100.0)	1,280 (100.0)
Men	1,632 (100.0)	1,963 (100.0)	2,210 (100.0)	2,479 (100.0)	2,519 (100.0)
Agriculture and Forestry					
Total employees	94 (4.0)	59 (2.1)	29 (0.9)	29 (0.8)	30 (0.8)
Women	37 (5.0)	20 (2.2)	10 (0.9)	8 (0.7)	9 (0.7)
Men	57 (3.5)	39 (2.0)	20 (0.9)	21 (0.9)	21 (0.8)
Nonagricultural Industry					
Fisheries and aquaculture					
Total employees	26 (1.1)	24 (0.8)	18 (0.5)	17 (0.5)	16 (0.4)
Women	3 (0.4)	2 (0.2)	2 (0.2)	1 (0.1)	1 (0.1)
Men	23 (1.4)	22 (1.1)	16 (0.7)	16 (0.7)	14 (0.6)
Mining					
Total employees	42 (1.8)	29 (1.0)	18 (0.5)	15 (0.4)	15 (0.4)
Women	4 (0.5)	3 (0.3)	2 (0.2)	1 (0.1)	2 (0.2)
Men	38 (2.3)	25 (1.3)	16 (0.7)	14 (0.6)	13 (0.5)
Construction					
Total employees	198 (8.4)	268 (9.3)	305 (9.2)	377 (10.3)	403 (10.6)
Women	29 (3.9)	40 (4.4)	45 (4.1)	49 (4.2)	53 (4.1)
Men	169 (10.4)	228 (11.6)	260 (11.8)	327 (13.2)	351 (13.9)

TABLE 5 – *Continued*

	1960	1965	1970	1975	1978
Manufacturing					
Total employees	799 (33.7)	993 (34.5)	1,144 (34.6)	1,138 (31.2)	1,109 (29.2)
Women	269 (36.4)	333 (36.5)	390 (35.6)	361 (30.9)	382 (29.8)
Men	530 (32.5)	660 (33.6)	754 (34.1)	776 (31.3)	727 (28.9)
Group A					
Total employees	449 (18.9)	593 (20.6)	731 (22.1)	868 (23.8)	942 (24.8)
Women	166 (22.5)	239 (26.2)	314 (28.6)	361 (30.9)	403 (31.5)
Men	283 (17.3)	354 (18.0)	418 (18.9)	507 (20.5)	539 (21.4)
Group B					
Total employees	232 (9.8)	287 (10.0)	340 (10.3)	346 (9.5)	356 (9.4)
Women	26 (3.5)	31 (3.4)	43 (3.9)	42 (3.6)	40 (3.1)
Men	206 (12.6)	256 (13.0)	296 (13.4)	304 (12.3)	316 (12.5)
Services					
Total employees	388 (16.4)	465 (16.2)	558 (16.9)	659 (18.1)	729 (19.2)
Women	182 (24.7)	219 (24.0)	265 (24.2)	312 (26.7)	355 (27.7)
Men	206 (12.6)	246 (12.5)	294 (13.3)	346 (14.0)	374 (14.8)
Government					
Total employees	142 (6.0)	158 (5.5)	161 (4.9)	196 (5.4)	197 (5.2)
Women	23 (3.1)	25 (2.7)	25 (2.3)	31 (2.7)	35 (2.7)
Men	119 (7.3)	133 (6.8)	136 (6.2)	165 (6.7)	162 (6.4)

Source: Prime Minister's Office, *Labor Force Survey*, cited in Ministry of Labor, *Fujin Rōdō no Jitsujō*, pp. 44–45.

Notes: Figures in parentheses are percentages of employee cohort. Group A includes wholesale and retail trade, finance, insurance, and real estate. Group B includes transportation, communication, electricity, gas, and water supply.

TABLE 6

Number of Women Employees and Women as Percentage of All Employees, by Medium Industry Group

Industry	Number of Women employees (1,000 persons)			Increasing Rate (percentage)			Women as Percentage of All Employees		
	1960	1965	1970	1960–70	1960–65	1965–70	1960	1965	1970
Total	2,563	3,225	3,684	43.7	25.8	14.2	31.4	32.4	32.4
Food and tobacco manufactures	273	394	408	49.6	44.2	3.7	37.6	43.4	45.3
Textile mill products	783	783	631	-19.3	0	-19.3	68.0	65.7	62.6
Apparel and fabric products	183	247	298	62.5	34.5	20.8	63.2	68.0	71.0
Lumber and wood products	95	120	25	32.2	27.0	4.1	21.8	26.0	28.5
Furniture and fixtures	24	46	59	145.6	92.5	27.6	12.1	19.5	22.7
Pulp, paper, and allied	85	107	94	10.8	26.7	-12.5	32.0	33.8	31.1
Publishing, printing, and related	69	109	128	86.3	57.9	18.0	19.0	23.0	24.3
Chemical and related	119	149	157	32.5	25.0	6.0	23.8	25.5	25.3
Petroleum and coal products	6	5	8	30.5	-8.5	42.6	14.8	14.1	14.9
Rubber products	64	59	75	17.5	-8.0	27.6	41.2	39.4	39.9
Leather products, fur	19	30	27	44.4	62.0	-10.9	29.5	33.0	37.0
Stone, clay, glass, pottery	106	130	162	52.5	22.4	24.7	26.6	28.1	28.9
Iron, steel, and nonferrous metal	62	83	90	45.4	33.9	8.6	10.5	12.3	11.5
Fabricated metal products	98	138	214	119.6	41.5	55.2	16.8	17.7	20.2
Machinery and weapons	85	128	183	114.9	49.7	43.5	12.9	13.8	16.7
Electrical machinery, and supplies	245	333	568	131.9	35.9	70.7	36.8	37.5	43.3
Transportation equipment	60	85	135	123.1	41.6	57.5	10.7	12.3	14.5
Precision machine	51	86	114	121.4	66.9	32.7	29.3	36.9	40.7
Miscellaneous manufacturing	137	194	207	51.2	41.7	6.7	39.9	41.3	38.0

Source: Prime Minister's Office, *Population Census*, as cited in U.S., Department of Labor, *The Role and Status of Women Workers in the United States and Japan — A Joint United States–Japan Study* (Washington, D.C.: Government Printing Office, 1976), p. 212.

107

TABLE 7

Number of Employees and Percentage Distribution, by Sex and Occupation
(x 10,000 persons)

	1960	1965	1970	1975	1978
Total					
Total employees	2,273 (100.0)	2,783 (100.0)	3,306 (100.0)	3,646 (100.0)	3,796 (100.0)
Men	1,578 (100.0)	1,911 (100.0)	2,210 (100.0)	2,479 (100.0)	2,517 (100.0)
Women	695 (100.0)	873 (100.0)	1,096 (100.0)	1,167 (100.0)	1,279 (100.0)
Women as percentage of all employees	30.6	31.4	33.2	32.0	33.7
Professional and technical workers					
Total employees	180 (8.2)	202 (7.3)	246 (7.4)	304 (8.3)	329 (8.7)
Men	120 (7.9)	126 (6.6)	146 (6.6)	169 (6.8)	173 (6.9)
Women	60 (9.0)	76 (8.7)	100 (9.1)	135 (11.6)	156 (12.2)
Women as percentage of all employees	33.3	37.6	40.7	44.4	47.4
Managers and Officials					
Total employees	79 (3.6)	116 (4.2)	131 (4.0)	204 (5.6)	201 (5.3)
Men	78 (5.1)	111 (5.8)	127 (5.7)	193 (7.8)	192 (7.6)
Women	2 (0.3)	4 (0.5)	5 (0.5)	11 (0.9)	9 (0.7)
Women as percentage of all employees	2.5	3.4	3.8	5.4	4.5
Clerical and related workers					
Total employees	474 (21.6)	629 (22.6)	723 (21.9)	776 (21.3)	819 (21.6)
Men	304 (20.0)	378 (19.8)	384 (17.4)	400 (16.1)	410 (16.3)
Women	170 (25.4)	251 (28.8)	339 (30.9)	376 (32.2)	409 (32.0)
Women as percentage of all employees	35.9	39.9	46.9	48.5	50.0

TABLE 7 — Continued

	1960	1965	1970	1975	1978
Sales workers					
Total employees	167 (7.6)	238 (8.6)	344 (10.4)	428 (11.8)	470 (12.4)
Men	109 (7.2)	151 (7.9)	231 (10.5)	299 (12.0)	322 (12.8)
Women	58 (8.7)	88 (10.1)	112 (10.2)	129 (11.1)	148 (11.6)
Women as percentage of all employees	34.7	37.0	32.6	30.2	31.5
Farmers, lumbermen, and fishermen					
Total employees	73 (3.3)	59 (2.1)	42 (1.3)	41 (1.1)	40 (1.1)
Men	49 (3.2)	44 (2.3)	32 (1.4)	32 (1.3)	31 (1.2)
Women	24 (3.6)	14 (1.6)	10 (0.9)	9 (0.8)	9 (0.7)
Women as percentage of all employees	32.9	23.7	23.8	22.0	22.5
Mining and quarrying workers					
Total employees	35 (1.6)	20 (0.7)	10 (0.3)	9 (0.3)	7 (0.2)
Men	33 (2.2)	19 (1.0)	9 (0.4)	9 (0.4)	7 (0.3)
Women	2 (0.3)	1 (0.1)	1 (0.1)	0 (0.0)	0 (0.0)
Women as percentage of all employees	5.7	5.0	10.0	0.0	0.0
Transport and communications workers					
Total employees	95 (4.3)	184 (6.6)	219 (6.6)	220 (6.0)	226 (5.9)
Men	89 (5.8)	162 (8.5)	197 (8.9)	203 (8.2)	212 (8.4)
Women	5 (0.7)	22 (2.5)	22 (2.0)	17 (1.5)	14 (1.1)
Women as percentage of all employees	5.3	12.0	10.0	7.7	6.2

TABLE 7 — *Continued*

	1960	1965	1970	1975	1978
Craftsmen and production process workers					
Total employees	892 (40.7)*	882 (31.7)	1,123 (34.0)	1,216 (33.4)	1,232 (32.4)
Men	652 (42.8)*	666 (34.6)	831 (37.6)	929 (37.5)	919 (36.5)
Women	240 (35.9)*	220 (25.2)	291 (26.6)	287 (24.6)	313 (24.5)
Women as percentage of all employees	26.9*	24.9	25.9	23.6	25.4
Laborers					
Total employees	892 (40.7)*	222 (8.0)	199 (6.0)	131 (3.6)	141 (3.7)
Men	652 (42.8)*	152 (8.0)	133 (6.0)	88 (3.6)	91 (3.6)
Women	240 (35.9)*	70 (8.0)	66 (6.0)	43 (3.7)	50 (3.9)
Women as percentage of all employees	26.9*	31.5	33.2	32.6	35.5
Service workers					
Total employees	197 (9.0)	232 (8.3)	267 (8.1)	315 (8.6)	331 (8.7)
Men	89 (5.8)	105 (5.5)	117 (5.3)	155 (6.3)	160 (6.4)
Women	108 (16.1)	127 (14.5)	150 (13.7)	160 (13.7)	171 (13.4)
Women as percentage of all employees	54.8	54.7	56.2	50.8	51.7

Source: Prime Minister's Office, *Labor Force Survey,* cited in Ministry of Labor, *Fujin Rōdō no Jitsujō,* pp. 46–47.

Note: No adjustment is made in figures from 1960 and 1965.

*Combined figure for the category for craftsmen and production process workers and the category for laborers.

TABLE 8

Number of Women Employees and Paid Employment Rate, by Marital Status

	Total	Single	Married	Widowed and Divorced
Employees (x 10,000 persons)				
1962	802	443	262	96
1965	893	449	345	99
1970	1,086	524	450	112
1975	1,159	440	595	125
1978	1,271	436	704	131
Percentage				
1962	100.0	55.2	32.7	12.0
1965	100.0	50.3	38.6	11.1
1970	100.0	48.3	41.4	10.3
1975	100.0	38.0	51.3	10.8
1978	100.0	34.3	55.4	10.3

Source: Prime Minister's Office, *Labor Force Survey*, cited in Ministry of Labor, *Fujin Rōdō no Jitsujō*, p. 51.

TABLE 9

Average Age and Average Length of Service, by Sex
(Size of establishment: 10 or more employees)

	Average Age			Average Length of Service (years)		
	Total	Women	Men	Total	Women	Men
1954	31.3	25.4	33.2	6.3	3.6	7.2
1960	30.9	26.3	32.8	6.7	4.0	7.8
1965	31.7	28.1	33.2	6.6	3.9	7.8
1970	33.2	30.2	34.5	7.4	4.4	8.2
1975	35.2	32.9	36.1	8.7	5.4	10.0
1978	36.3	34.1	37.2	9.7	6.1	11.1

Source: Ministry of Labor, *Basic Survey of Wage Structure*, cited in Ministry of Labor, *Fujin Rōdō no Jitsujō*, p. 54.

TABLE 10

Number of Employees Working Fewer than 35 Hours a Week in Nonagricultural Industry, by Sex
(x 10,000 persons)

	1960	1965	1970	1975	1978
All employees					
Total	2,106	2,713	3,222	3,556	3,715
Employees working fewer than 35 hours	133 (6.3)	178 (6.6)	216 (6.7)	353 (9.9)	330 (8.9)
Women					
Total	639	851	1,068	1,137	1,251
Employees working fewer than 35 hours	57 (8.9)	82 (9.6)	130 (12.2)	198 (17.4)	215 (17.2)
Men					
Total	1,467	1,862	2,154	2,419	2,464
Employees working fewer than 35 hours	76 (5.2)	96 (5.2)	86 (4.0)	155 (6.4)	115 (4.7)

Source: Prime Minister's Office, *Labor Force Survey*, cited in Ministry of Labor, *Fujin Rōdō no Jitsujō*, p. 56.

Note: Figures in parentheses are the percentages of total employees in category.

TABLE 11

Average Monthly Cash Earnings, by Sex
(size of establishment: 30 or more employees)

		Total Cash Earnings	Contractual Cash Earnings	Special Cash Payments	Differentials between Women and Men (men = 100)		
					A	B	C
		(in yen)					
1955	Total	18,343	15,741	2,602			
	Women	9,479	8,229	1,250	44.4	45.4	40.7
	Men	21,349	18,277	3,072			
1960	Total	24,375	19,617	4,758			
	Women	12,414	10,129	2,285	42.8	43.5	39.9
	Men	29,029	23,303	5,726			
1965	Total	39,360	30,936	8,421			
	Women	22,275	17,760	4,515	47.8	48.7	44.8
	Men	46,571	36,496	10,075			
1970	Total	75,670	56,294	19,376			
	Women	45,801	34,482	11,319	50.9	51.7	48.7
	Men	89,934	66,710	23,224			
1975	Total	177,213	130,004	47,209			
	Women	144,067	84,431	29,636	55.8	56.5	54.1
	Men	204,295	149,549	54,746			
1978	Total	235,378	174,739	60,639			
	Women	152,420	113,624	38,796	56.2	56.5	55.4
	Men	271,125	201,071	70,050			

Source: Ministry of Labor, *Monthly Labor Survey*, cited in Ministry of Labor, *Fujin Rōdō no Jitsujō*, p. 71.

Notes: A. Total cash earnings. B. Contractual cash earnings. C. Special cash payments. Figures for 1970 include services.

TABLE 12
Starting Wages of New Graduates, by Sex
(in yen)

	1960	1965	1970	1975	1978
Junior high school					
Women	5,590	13,330	23,100	55,400	57,400
Men	5,910	13,190	23,800	58,000	62,500
*Differential between sexes	94.6	101.1	97.1	95.5	91.8
Senior high school					
Women	7,300	15,670	26,400	66,300	72,900
Men	8,160	16,430	28,400	70,400	75,600
Differential between sexes	89.5	95.4	93.0	94.2	96.4
University					
Women	12,520	21,740	34,500	78,800	86,100
Men	13,080	22,980	37,400	83,600	91,700
Differential between sexes	95.7	94.6	83.7	94.3	93.9

Source: Ministry of Labor, *White Paper on Labor*, 1979, appendix 48.

*Men = 100.0.

TABLE 13

Differentials between Women and Men in Average Monthly Earnings, by Age (Men = 100.0)

		Age											
		17	18–19	20–24	25–29	30–34	35–39	40–44	45–49	50–54	55–59	60–64	65+
1954	Contractual cash earnings	102.0	81.7	71.0	61.1	47.1	40.5	37.0		36.0			40.5
1960	Contractual cash earnings	99.6	79.1	68.6	61.4	50.7		—		—			—
1965	Contractual cash earnings	96.5	83.1	71.5	61.0	53.5	47.9	41.5		43.2			52.6
	Regular cash earnings	97.8	88.8	78.2	67.1	58.1	52.1	44.7		46.0			54.2
1970	Contractual cash earnings	91.8	79.9	72.4	60.0	47.2	44.3	42.9		45.1			59.8
	Regular cash earnings	92.5	87.2	79.5	66.6	52.6	48.7	46.5		48.5			62.7
1975	Contractual cash earnings	91.6	86.5	78.8	67.7	54.8	47.6	46.0	47.5	46.8	53.4		64.1
	Regular cash earnings	92.3	90.7	83.4	71.9	58.3	50.1	48.3	49.8	48.5	55.2		65.9
1978	Contractual cash earnings	91.3	86.3	80.9	69.0	56.8	48.9	45.3	47.8	49.5	54.5	66.6	71.4
	Regular cash earnings	91.4	93.2	87.2	74.6	61.3	52.5	48.1	50.6	52.1	56.7	68.9	73.5

Source: Ministry of Labor, *Basic Survey of Wage Structure*, cited in Ministry of Labor, *Fujin Rōdō no Jitsujō*, p. 74.

Bibliography

Abegglen, James. *Japanese Factory.* New York: Free Press, 1958.

Akamatsu, Ryōko, ed. *Joshi Rōdō Hanrei* [Decisions on women workers]. Tokyo: Gakuyōshobō, 1976.

——. *Nihon Fujin Mondai Shiryoshusei* [Collection of materials on Japanese women's problems]. Vol. 3, Labor. Tokyo: Domesu Shuppan, 1977.

Asahi Shinbun, April 8, 1972.

Cole, Robert E. *Japanese Blue Collar: The Changing Tradition.* Berkeley: University of California Press, 1971.

Cook, Alice H. *An Introduction to Japanese Trade Unionism.* Ithaca: New York State School of Industrial and Labor Relations, Cornell University, 1966.

——. *The Working Mother.* 2d ed., rev. Ithaca: New York State School of Industrial and Labor Relations, Cornell University, 1978.

Dore, Robert. *British Factory–Japanese Factory: The Origins of National Diversity in Industrial Relations.* Berkeley: University of California Press, 1973.

Fujin Rōdō Mondai Kenkyūkai (Study Group on Working Women's Problems). *Gendai no Fujin Rōdō Mondai* [The problems of present-day working women]. Tokyo: Rōdō Jumpōsha, 1975.

Hanami, Tadashi. *Labor Relations in Japan Today.* Tokyo: Kōdansha International, 1979.

Hayashi, Hiroko. "The Litigating Tactics by Working Women: Coping with the Gap between Legal Norm and Social Norm." Paper prepared for the International Sociological Congress, section on women's movements, Uppsala, Sweden, August 13, 1978.

Bibliography

Higuchi, Yukiko, and Sakamoto, Fukuko. *Hataraku Fujin no Kenri to Tatakai* [The struggle for working women's rights]. Tokyo: Minshusha, 1976.

International Labour Organisation. "Health Protection of Women Workers." Processed. Tokyo: International Labour Organisation, [1973?].

Japan Institute of Labour. *Japan Labour Statistics*. Tokyo: Japan Institute of Labour, 1974.

Japan, Ministry of Labor. "Working Women's Welfare Law" (provisional translation). Law no. 113 of 1972. Tokyo: Ministry of Labor, 1973.

Japan, Ministry of Labor, Women's and Minors' Bureau. *Fujin no Ayumi 30 Nen* [Thirty years' women's progress]. Tokyo: Rōdō Horei Kyokai, 1975.

——. *Fujin Rōdō Hōsei no Kadai to Hōkō —Rōkiho Kenkyūkai Hōkoku* [The problem and trend of the legal protection of women workers—the report of the Labor Standards Law Research Society]. Tokyo: Nikkan Rōdō Thōshinsha, 1978.

——. *Fujin Rōdō no Jitsujō* [Facts on women's labor]. Tokyo: Finance Ministry Printing office, 1979.

——. *Shokuba ni Okeru Danjo Byodo o Susumemashō* [Let's implement equal working conditions between men and women]. Pamphlet 78. Tokyo: Ministry of Labor, 1979.

——. *Status of Women in Japan*. Tokyo: Ministry of Labor, 1974, 1977, 1978.

Japan, Prime Minister's Office, Commission for the Planning and Promotion of Policies Relating to Women in Japan. *National Plan of Action* (tentative translation). Tokyo: Prime Minister's Office, 1977.

Japan Times, December 11, 1971.

Levine, Solomon. *Industrial Relations in Postwar Japan*. Urbana: University of Illinois, 1958.

Marsh, Robert M., and Nannari, Hiroshi. *Modernization and the Japanese Factory*. Princeton: Princeton University Press, 1976.

Bibliography

Matsuoka, Saburō, *Fujin Nenshō Rōdō* [Women's and minors' labor]. Tokyo: Sōgō Rōdō Kenkyūsho, 1979.

Moriyama, Mayumi. "Women Workers in Japan." Paper prepared for the International Symposium on Women and Industrial Relations, Vienna, September 12–15, 1978.

Nakane, Chie. *Japanese Society.* Berkeley and Los Angeles: University of California Press, 1970.

Nihon Koku Kempō, *Byōdōken* [Right of equality]. Tokyo: Sanseidō, 1977.

Ōkōchi, Kazuo; Karsh, Bernard; and Levine, Solomon B. *Workers and Employers in Japan: The Japanese Employment Relations System.* Princeton: Princeton University Press, 1973.

Organisation for Economic Cooperation and Development. "Manpower and Social Affairs Committee, the Role of Women in the Economy," in *National Report, Japan.* Processed. Paris: Organisation for Economic Cooperation and Development, 1973.

Ōwaki, Masako, "Nissan Jidōsha Sabetsu Teinensei Hanketsu no Igi to Mondaiten" [The meaning of the decision on discrimination on retirement age in the Nissan Automobile Company]. *Jurist* 695 (1979).

———. "Maternity Protection as an Excuse for Discrimination," *Feminist* 6 (1978).

Sangyo Rōdō Chōsasho. *Rōkihō Kaisei Mondai to Jyoshi Hogo — Rōkihō Kenkyūkai Hōkoku ni Tsuite no Rōshi no Iken* [Issues on the revision of the Labor Standards Law and protection of women workers — the opinions of management and labor]. Tokyo: Sangyō Rōdō Chōsasho, 1979.

Shimada, Nobuyoshi. *Hataraku Fujin no Kenri Tokuhon* [Book of rights of working women]. Tokyo: Rōdō Jumpōsha, 1975.

———. "Seirikyūka no Mukyūka Keiko to Seikyūken no Yōgo" [Trend of making menstrual leave unpaid and the case for the right to menstrual leave], *Rōdō Hōritsu Jumpō* 860 (1974).

Bibliography

Sumiya, Mikio. "Rinjiko Mondai no Genjō" [The present stage of the issue of temporary employees] *Nihon Rōdō Kyōkai Zasshi* 5:3 (March 1963).

Taira, Kōji. *Economic Development and Labor Markets in Japan.* New York: Columbia University Press, 1970.

U.S., Department of Labor, Bureau of Labor Standards. *U.S. Working Women: A Data Book.* Washington, D.C.: Government Printing Office, 1977.

U.S., Department of Labor, Employment Standards Administration, Women's Bureau. *The Role and Status of Women Workers in the United States and Japan — A Joint United States – Japan Study.* Washington, D.C.: Government Printing Office, 1976.

Yakabe, Katsumi. *Labor Relations in Japan.* Tokyo: International Society for Educational Information, 1978.

In addition to the sources listed here, the following periodicals offer information pertinent to the subject of working women in Japan: *Japanese Women,* semiannual newsletter published by Fusenkai; *Japan Labor Bulletin,* published monthly by Japan Institute of Labour; *Jurist,* legal journal, published semimonthly by Yūhikaku; *Nihon Rōdō Kyōkai Zasshi,* published monthly by Japan Institute of Labour; and *Rōdō Hōrei Tsūshin* [Labor legislation news], published three times a month by Rōdō Hōrei Kyōkai; and *Rōdō Hōritsu Jumpō,* published three times a month by Rōdō Hōrtisu Jumpōsha.

Index

121

Index

Index

Part-time workers, 6–7, 11–12, 23, 52–55, 58, 97, 113; and unions, 7
Pensions, 23–24
Permanent workers, 7
Pregnancy, 45
Prime Minister's Office, 75, 82; Advisory Commission on Planning and Promotion of Policies Relating to Women, 75, 82, 86, 89–90, 92 n. 3
Promotion opportunity, 7, 29, 39, 43
Public employment, 8–9, 17–18, 79; discrimination cases in, 63–64; National Personnel Authority, 33 n. 25

Retirement, 22–29; early, 9–10, 25–29, 86; early, at age thirty, 57–58; early, at childbirth, 25; early, at marriage, 25, 46–51
Retirement age, 24–25, 28 (table 3), 34 n. 34, 58–59; difference between men and woman, 23, 24, 58–63, 86
Retirement policies, 24–29

Sanwa Bank, 52–53
Satō, Susumu, 68–69, 70
Semiskilled workers, 12
Seniority wage system, 25, 27, 28, 40, 42, 45, 48, 59
Senju Food Institute, 18
Shibata, Tomoko, 92 n. 3
Shiga, Suiko, 56
Shigehara City, 50
Shimizu, Mutsuko, 57–58
Shizouka Bank, 43
Shumpū-dō department store, 54–55
Socialist Party. *See* Japan Socialist Party

Sogyorōren, 85
Sōhyō, 19
Special allowance, 41
Status, 5, 35
Suenami, Kazumi, 51–52
Suit: original, 37–38; provisional, 37–38, 61, 65
Sumitomo Cement Company, 46–49
Supplementary workers, 47, 56, 59
Support organizations, 83
Supreme Court, 50; decisions, 50, 59–60
Suzuka City, 42, 43
Suzuki, Setsuko, 46–49

Tachinaka, Shūko, 64–65, 71
Takahashi, Hisako, 78, 92 n. 3
Tamaoki, Masako, 53–54
Tanaka, Michiko, 57–58
Tanaka, Sumiko, 87–89
Teachers, 17, 85
Teikoku Kōshin-jo Company, 73, 74
Temporary workers. *See* Part-time workers
Tokkyū Kikan Kōgyō, 55–57
Tōshiba Kikai Company, 40–41
Tōshiba Yanigimachi Plant, 54–55
Tōyō Kōhan, 64–65, 71
Tōyō Seiki, 53–55
Trade Union Act, 67
Trade union conference, 18
Trade union federation, 19
Training, 9, 16, 28, 87
Transfer, 63; cases involving, 63–67
Tsukamoto General Industries, 67

Unions, 7, 19–20, 24, 75, 91; in discrimination cases, 40, 41, 43, 55, 61, 72–73, 83–85; activity protected, 66. *See* Collective agreements

123

Index